IMPERMANENCE
IMPERMANENCE
IMPERMANENCE
IMPERMANENCE
IMPERMANENCE
IMPERMANENCE
IMPERMANENCE
IMPERMANENCE
IMPERMANENCE
IMPERMANENCE
IMPERMANENCE
IMPERMANENCE
IMPERMANENCE
IMPERMANENCE
IMPERMANENCE

EDITED BY NEIL HEGARTY AND NORA HICKEY M'SICHILI

NO ALIBIS PRESS / CENTRE CULTUREL IRLANDAIS

First published in 2022
by No Alibis Press in collaboration
with the Centre Culturel Irlandais

Printed by Walsh Colour Print, Kerry

Book design: Stephen Connolly

A CIP record for this book
is available from the British Library

ISBN 978-1838108199

2 4 6 8 10 9 7 5 3 1

Contents

Preface

This collection of essays originated in a series of conversations about permanence—or rather, impermanence. Indeed, these conversations were backlit by impermanence. The spring of 2020: and the Covid emergency was still running at full throttle, with the shape of all our lives a good deal less solid than had been the case eighteen months earlier. Our cities were being remade, our work lives reshaped, our family ties stretched by months of distance and isolation—and habits and casts of mind that had seemed fixed and unvarying had been cracked, broken, and remade. Old patterns were being sloughed off, and new ones were in the process of being created.

There was a further element in this backlit context. The centenary of Irish partition was upon us: and given its role as a focus of Irish culture in Europe, the Centre Culturel Irlandais was keen to provide a space to reflect on how this fraught anniversary was being approached, and how it was to be commemorated and addressed. Brexit had spectacularly queered this particular pitch: after all, the Good Friday Agreement had appeared to offer a form of imperfect settlement to the Irish question; but now, a note of impermanence had been added to both present and future, with the matter of Irish unity up for newly energetic debate. The tectonic plates were shifting in a way that would have appeared unimaginable just a decade ago.

Our very natural human tendency is to invest in images of stability: the home and the roof over our heads; our relationships and the bonds of love that we like to think of as unbreakable; the built environment that surrounds us and that influences our lives so profoundly; the states and nations within which we live and to which we contribute in manifold ways. We invest emotionally in such images, even though—or because—they carry the hallmark of an essential impermanence. We live in the moment and imagine its permanence, even though each moment is vanishing as it is being experienced, slipping into the next moment, and the next.

Culture and politics and creativity: our lives and experiences are composed not of some intrinsic stability— but rather of impermanence, and of impermanences. Our homes and relationships, work and love, circumstances and breaks lucky and unlucky, our very characters and emotions: these are inevitably provisional, always flowing, always leading elsewhere. And nations are provisional too, of course: a glance at history, at our present moment in Europe, at the ever-altering maps of the continent through the ages, at personal testimony and at archival material, will remind us that we exist in a state of permanent flux. We must build anew throughout the course of our lives—lives that are lived out in that state of transience known in Buddhist traditions as the bardo.

Neuroscience has of late taught us that we understand and absorb this unavoidable fact of transience at cellular level: that this wisdom is embedded into the architecture of our brain—which, rather than being fixed or set, is able to fire and adapt and construct new neural pathways until the moment of death. Our minds work with an impermanent grain, for all that our emotions appear to militate against a recognition of the fact. We are designed to accept an impermanent way, and to embrace its possibilities.

In the course of one conversation—and the better to illustrate the state of impermanence against which our lives are lived—we were reminded of certain vivid images and common memories which sprang from our childhoods in the Northern Ireland of the 1970s. A display noticed and appreciated in a shop window, or a shop visited and its wares admired—but within days, the shop, its windows, its wares are gone, erased, bombed during the night. This happened again and again: it was an all too common experience of those troubled times. We reflected that not only did such smoke-filled vignettes illustrate very well the psychic tension and trauma that accompanied daily life in the midst of the Troubles, but that such disturbing incidents appear to reset or rewire in a certain way the sensibilities of those who witness them: that having lived through such history, in which the stuff of our lives are—

manifestly, terrifyingly—shown to be impermanent, one is more likely to accept, even to embrace the principle of impermanence.

And we also reflected on the context of our first conversation, which had taken place in the physical setting of the Centre Culturel Irlandais on a fine, warm afternoon in April 2019. Later that same afternoon, the air filled with smoke—and on the crest of the hill nearby, Parisians gathered to watch in shocked silence as Notre Dame, for almost a thousand years a seemingly permanent emblem of the city of Paris, burned on the island below.

As the result of our backlit conversations, then, the idea has taken shape: a collection of writings on the theme of impermanence, that central fact and sensation of each of our lives, and of our histories, and our futures. We invited our contributors to range freely, widely, in their responses: to frame these responses in terms personal, environmental, philosophical, architectural; in terms of personal, private, archival or public history. The result is a collection that explores the texture of impermanence and of change—and the possibilities that flow from this awareness of transience.

Neil Hegarty and Nora Hickey M'Sichili
Dublin and Paris, May 2022

Like Leaves, Like Sand
Brian McGilloway

When we were children, my parents would take me, my
sister and my two brothers from Derry into Donegal for
what was colloquially known as a 'run'. This was not a
wholly accurate description, for it was more of a drive,
the bulk of the day being spent in a car. We'd a five-
seater estate car to accommodate six of us: a state of affairs
which necessitated my being put into the boot where I
would roll around as the car took each bend in the road
from Derry to Buncrana. No talk of seat belts or booster
cushions then. The journey required us to cross the
Irish border from North to South, albeit that we were,
incongruously, heading northwards to achieve this feat.
I remember those crossings—driving through a military
installation where young squaddies cradling rifles like
their new-born infants, would wave down my father and,
with a twirl of their gloved fingers, indicate he should
wind down the window. The car would be sweet and
heady with the smell of the tobacco he smoked—Condor
Longcut—his pipe stem clamped between his teeth as he
waited to play his part in the weekly routine:

Where were we going?

Why?

How long would we stay?

Did he have his licence?

What was the registration number of the car?

That final one would be followed by the soldier stepping in front of the car to check if my father was right, then moving on to check the back, for further authentication, in case the vehicle was stolen. As they rounded the boot, sometimes they would look in to where I squatted, and they'd wink, or smile, or sometimes neither. They were of a different world to me, their accents, their uniforms, their authority over even my father. Sometimes they would make us drive across to a hangar to search the car: but usually they would wave us on.

Weather allowing, we'd stop at one of the beaches along the Inishowen coastline, most often Fahan. There, for the first time, 'run' would become a more accurate reflection of events as my brothers and I, freed from the car, would set off along the beach, skirting the water's edge, picking our way over rocks, running up the sand dunes, pushing through the sharp-bladed marram grass and launching ourselves back down onto the beach below, rolling through the sand before beginning once more.

The journey down from the dunes was easy, though fraught with the potential for injury or collision with an older sibling. But climbing back up was not so simple.

The sand, fine and fluid, would collapse under each step as I tried to make my way back up the dune. The ground would slide from beneath me, the appearance of solidity giving way as my foot touched the surface and the sand funnelled into the gap created by my weight. The very act of trying to find anything other than the most temporary foothold hastened the dune's collapse, its impermanence mocking anyone who tried to stay too long in one spot.

The nature of the dune was transitory. The trick was to find the firmer sand, the sand that would not give. But you could never find such sand so far from the water. I would step and the ground would leave me, over and over, until I lost my balance and, falling forwards, would scrabble for purchase or reach out for a brother to pull me up to safer ground and a more solid footing once more.

Such days seemed to last forever. Our childhood, even against the context of the Troubles, was one of happiness and relative peace, in no small measure due to the efforts of my mother and father to shield us from the worst effects of the violence and the worst extremes of the sectarian hatred which stalked the country then and whose shadow stretches still.

My parents did not seem to age, even as we, children, did. Primary school gave way to secondary school. My sister went to university; I remember the day she left, remember the tears in the house and the excitement. The same again when my eldest brother went and again with the next. Then, finally, my own exams, GCSE and A

Level, then my leave-taking to go to college. We seemed to be growing up, but my parents did not change. Or if they did, it was so incremental as not to be noticeable to me.

Or else, I was just a teenager, my world revolving around myself, my friends, my interests.

Of a sudden, time seemed to move more quickly, each year measured by milestones. First car, first job, engagement, marriage, a new home, a baby, another, another, another, a family, a large car—a seven-seater. Going for a run with my own children.

My wife Tanya's pregnancy with our first child brought with it the realisation that my life was altering in seismic ways, in ways for which I did not feel prepared. And I recall, in particular, the growing awareness that any sense of control I'd had, was illusory.

In response, I did the only reasonable thing I could—I wrote a book. Featuring a character with a young baby, a detective who patrols the borderlands of Ireland and brings order to a chaotic world, I have no doubt that the creative impulse which I'd always felt, was, in this case, propelled by my recognition of my inability to control the real world, catalysing my taking control of a fictional one instead. It was the first time I understood at a personal level that art is an act of defiance against our powerlessness in the face of a chaotic and, ultimately, transitory, existence.

As my children grew, so too did those of my fictional

counterpart, Ben Devlin. And, as I struggled with and learnt how to be a parent, so too did he, trying his best, frequently failing, but always reflecting my concerns about the world. And he aged with me—something that was more reflected in the changes in his children than in himself.

This was because, at some point, I realised that the milestones marking out the passing of time were now all my children's, not mine any longer. Christenings, First Communions, Confirmations, all the ceremonies with which we formalise their growth. My life seemed to slow—or perhaps I simply became less selfish as I watched my children grow and develop, taking joy with them in each new experience, but with a feeling that time had set itself in abeyance for me.

And, as my children's growth now seemed to accelerate even as mine appeared to have slowed, so too did my parents slow. Perhaps it was the awareness of the growing contrast between my children and my parents—as one stretched the other seemed to shrink, the embrace of one strengthened while the other weakened. And I remained between the two—one of the so-called sandwich generation—acutely aware of the insidiousness of time but seemingly free of its effects personally.

I think it is in part because the milestones that mark the movement of early adulthood bring with them their own self-awareness of growth and maturation. A house, a job, a wife, a child. Each carry with them a liminality where we feel we have moved forward, grown up, as we pass through them. Each marks out a moment as before and after: life single, life married; life without children, life with. Each change changes us.

But in 'middle parenthood', each day is the same, each week bleeding one into the next, each year a succession of school sports days and childhood sicknesses, nativity plays and summer holidays. There we find the numbing quality of habit—the great deadener, as Beckett said. For a moment, we believe time has stalled, that this might be permanent, that the dune has been mastered, the solid ground found.

The sickness and the loss of my father shattered that conception for me. Partly, it was because it was one of those milestones which, by its nature, reflected the implacability of time. It was impossible to go back, even for a second, to before that moment, except in either memory or dream.

And that engendered in me a deep longing to see him again. To touch his hand, hear his voice, to embrace him. I can still see his hands, clasped in mine, can *almost* feel the touch of them, the roughness of his skin, his warmth. Almost. It is, as if, just beyond my fingertips, as if, if I stretched far enough, I could brush against that moment once more and recapture it for a second. But that moment is irrecoverable and, even as I try to hold the sensation in my mind, it already slips from me, like the sand beneath my feet as I climbed that childhood dune, the grains slipping through the hourglass of the years.

Since my father's death, my own children, seemingly infants forever, have changed in ways that have caught me by surprise, even as such changes were inevitable. One of them is taller than me now, one has left to go to university. They've all completed primary school, all completed those early ceremonies with our daughter's Confirmation this year.

I feel increasingly as if I have stepped into my own father's shoes, that only now do I understand what he must have felt, the passing of time, each heartbeat a metronomic pulse.

The past few years have reinforced for me the idea, always present but not, until recently, real for me, that life is a slow but constant process of letting go. As we grow, our own parents had to let go of us—indeed, like every parent, had in effect spent all their efforts in teaching us how to continue without them. Simultaneously, as parents ourselves, we had prepared our own children to move on beyond us. It is a strange irony that the measure of success as a parent is the level of preparedness that our children have for leaving us. And that is just and right— for we are all, ultimately, children of time and all of our relationships carry with them the sadness of knowing that nothing can last forever. That all things—and all people—must some day pass.

The final lesson our parents teach us is how to let them go.

And yet when I think back to those childhood runs to Donegal, I am aware of how different a world it was to that which my children now know in ways that go beyond the familial. We cross the border frequently now and the transition is marked by no more than a difference in the quality of the tar used to surface the road and the speed signs changing from MPH to KPH. Strangely, my own personal reminder of how loss, how letting go of old certainties is a central part of life, has unfolded alongside a wider societal shaking loose of things which had, for so long, seemed permanent and unmoveable.

I was born in 1974 in Derry. I knew my tribe, knew my identity, knew the name I called the city, which country I belonged to, not because it was forced on me by my parents, but because that was what was required in such a society.

Where are you from?

The answer would tell your audience your political and religious affiliations, would allow them to make suppositions about you as a person, just as it had when the squaddie at the checkpoint had asked my father where he was coming from.

Answering that one simple question forced you to self-identify in so many ways: I knew where the border lay, knew the resentment, passed through generations, that my home had been scarred by this line. Like all of those who lived through such days, our childhood news reports were a catalogue of the latest atrocities. Frequently, a slow haemorrhaging, one or two lives lost every week—sometimes a bloodletting with casualties in double figures or higher. But it seemed interminable, a fact of life in Northern Ireland, a repetition of history which was increasingly tragic, never farcical, a perpetual and self-perpetuating war, each generation made in the mould of the previous, taught its hatreds and prejudices at birth. It seemed that it would never end—that we were cursed to tear ourselves apart for eternity.

Yet, change came—slowly, but it did still come. And, with the Good Friday Agreement, and the new hope it brought, some of the old certainties began to crumble. Most obviously for those of us who lived near the border, the military installations which had been a permanent feature of our youth vanished—almost overnight in some cases. That which had seemed permanent and unmoveable was suddenly gone from our vision and with it flourished the incipient hope that if it could go, what else might change.

The border was still there, still existed, but was invisible and did not impede daily life in any noticeable way for most of us. We had reached a new normal where the cosmetic features of our past had gone while the border itself remained, albeit, beyond our sight, unless we choose to see it—substance conferred by acknowledgement in a type of Berkeley-esque fashion. The change brought with it relative peace, if not always stability. But certainly it was a significant improvement over how we had lived for thirty plus years. And so it would remain, it seemed.

Then, a discussion around Brexit in Britain, spilled over to us here. Its most vocal supporters in the north were the very politicians who most wanted to retain the border and saw Brexit as a way to reinforce it, make it more permanent as we approached the centenary of its inception. But this showed a failure or an unwillingness to grasp that the border had continued to exist following the peace process precisely because it had become less substantial. That many in the middle ground would continue to accept it existed on the basis that they could pretend that it didn't. Its visible absence allowed the old tribal identities to weaken, allowed people to self-identify with a combination of nationalities.

If there is no line, there is no need to work out on which side of it you stand, after all.

Brexit hardened once more the psychological border for everyone living along it and seemed to threaten those whose self-identity had an element of the European. We were confronted once more with the potential tangible effects of the frontier's reinforcement, whether physical or legislative, something which, in turn, encouraged the reemergence of tribalism. It was an act that ran contrary to the spirit of the Good Friday Agreement which worked to overcome tribalist thinking. Ironically, those who advocated for Brexit on this island were, primarily, from the two extremes of both tribes who clearly believed that the reinforcement of the border would act as a recruitment agent for their diametrically opposed aims. The majority, in the middle, were happy to continue as we had until enough time passed, and demographics changed, that the old lines would fade. Transition points are, by their nature, transitory, after all. Some could content themselves in believing the border was permanent—others could tell themselves it was temporary, a juggling act achieved by the Good Friday Agreement and either forgotten or disregarded by the architects of Brexit.

Instead, we had something foisted on us which we did not want, had not sought and did not vote for. I recall the morning the Brexit result was announced, the sense of shock, the fear that all that we had achieved here, all that we had created as a shared society had been built on sand and was now being torn down as a result of the internal wrangling of a political party in Britain. Those who supported it celebrated, claiming the act would lead to the reinforcement of the union, would prove that we were better together, even as they marked a vote which they had fought on the grounds that we were better apart, as if leaving one union would prove the value in reinforcing another.

The issue was, that the Brexit vote had shown that old political certainties were impermanent. Brexit showed that the unchanging political order of the previous forty years could be changed, challenged, overturned. That unions could be broken. And it created disorder where, for a while at least, there had been a sense of order.

And, as with my own experience as a new father, chaos spurs compulsion.

Except, in this case, we see a hardening of political rhetoric now, old enmities flaring once more on the extremes, street protests and threats of violence enflamed, if not outright encouraged, by those who would abdicate all responsibility for having created the chaos through their own short-sighted attempts to reclaim a 'glorious' past. There is a sense that with the old certainties crumbling, some wish to grip them ever tighter, in the hope that they will hold, that the force of their conviction alone will be cement enough to secure them permanently.

But, like the hand of a lost parent, the urge to hold onto the very thing which made us, which gave us meaning, is impossible, no matter how deep the longing to do so or how terrible the grief on knowing that we cannot. We know this, have been told it before. From Heraclitus' 'You cannot step in the same river twice' to Fitzgerald's 'You can't repeat the past' to Wolfe's 'You can't go home again': literature is awash with the lesson that we are beholden to time and its nature. That ours is an impermanent way.

And yet, for me, literature is also our response to that very same knowledge—an act of wilful defiance against our own impermanence.

Last year, driven both by a reawakened awareness of the border and still struggling with the loss of my father, I wrote the first Devlin novel in almost a decade, returning to the border landscape which I had left behind in 2012. It was my own act of defiance, a way to capture something of the wisdom and spirit of my father—gentle, kind, unassuming—and hold it in a form more tangible than a dream.

And so, in that new Devlin, *Blood Ties*, Devlin's father is dying, as Covid rages and the fall-out of Brexit continues. It is a story of identity and grief, of family and all the things which make us who we are. Bringing those memories of my own father to life once more, in my imagination, forced me to face the lesson again: that ultimately, all is transitory, our way is an impermanent one, our path as insubstantial as a sand dune, giving way beneath us with each step, collapsing in our wake, never to be walked again by us in the same form.

Yet, while we cannot walk the same path twice, we can leave a guide for those who follow after us, a record of our journey, that they may learn and remember and share their own tales. For, while our directions may differ, when the dunes collapse, when the ground goes beneath us, Art, like the welcome grasp of a brother, guides us to the more solid ground.

Art understands the transitory nature of our existence, embraces it and, ironically, challenges it. Our way may be impermanent, but in capturing it through Art, we transcend that very impermanence, even as we create something insubstantial. Ozymandias's statue may have fallen in the poem of that name, but the words remain.

We are bound by time. Art is our only act of defiance, an expression of that which unites us in our common humanity, far beyond borders or Brexit. We still read the earliest epics, mythologies of cultures past, long collapsed now, because they connect with us on a human level. Their story is our story and creates a bond between us that time cannot destroy.

It is our cry, at once ephemeral and vital, against the very impermanence of our existence. And it is one which, like these words, echo on, even after the speaker has gone silent.

Only our words will remain.

We must hope they are enough.

Late August, Early September, 2021
Carlo Gébler

It was the last day of our August holiday. We were slightly gloomy on that account, plus, all week we'd been buffeted by the melancholy news from Afghanistan of the Taliban's relentless advance on Kabul, and only that morning we'd learnt they'd reached the capital's gates and stopped, an act of tact which supposedly was to be admired but which we suspected was ominous. If ever there was a day to visit Milk Harbour—we'd seen the sign on the Bundoran road for this magically named place numerous times but never turned—today was that day.

I turned off my phone—no more news—and off we set. At the fingerpost—it was the old-fashioned black-on-white kind from a John Hinde postcard—we turned and followed a narrow road to the end. Milk Harbour, built by the Congested Districts Board I guessed, was a stone-built beauty. Below the quays, foreshores buried under drifts of seaweed, and, lower still, between the foreshores, the sea, like a thread of mercury, smooth and silky and still. The tide was out. In the far west, a line of marram grass-covered dunes. All in all, the full John Hinde.

We walked away along the foreshore until my wife spotted them on the opposite shore: a heron, stock still on a single leg, a bull seal, heavy, dark, monarchical, two female seals with glorious pelts, and three seal pups, shiny and black.

We sat down to observe. The seals lifted their heads and stared back but did not move. The sky turned lilac. Swallows flittered so close we heard their wings whirring.

After an hour, a liquorice head popped out of the water—a fourth pup. It wriggled up beside its siblings. In the distance, against the far dunes, horses cantered.

'Where are those dunes?' wondered my wife.

Apple Maps would know, I thought. I turned on my phone. It pulsed and a box shimmered into view before the password request: in the last hour, whilst we'd sat with the seals, the Taliban had given up waiting. They were flooding into Kabul.

Well, I'd opened the damned phone, I thought, so now I damn well had to finish. The dunes, I discovered, were on Conors Island and along the back of Streedagh Strand.

The evening bulletins were dismal. One commentator bracketed Kabul's fall with Paris's in 1940. I went to bed but couldn't sleep. About 2 a.m. I got up and went to the sitting room. The dark beyond the windows was sepulchral. I picked up W.G. Sebald's *The Rings of Saturn*, which I'd brought to read but hadn't started. I opened it and saw Chapter Five included Irish content. That'll do I thought.

Chapter Five narrated with phenomenal dexterity the stories of Joseph Conrad, son of Polish nationalists, first a British merchant marine officer, later a writer; and Roger Casement, son of Ulster Protestants, first a British civil servant who exposed the terrible things happening to the indigenous peoples in Belgium's Congo colony (this was where Casement met Conrad) and then in the jungle areas of Peru, Colombia and Brazil, later an Irish nationalist committed to armed struggle against Britain. In 1916 Casement was arrested and put in the Tower of London. His house was searched and Black Diaries were found that chronicled his homosexual relationships. In the run-up to his treason trial, the Black Diaries' incendiary contents were leaked to the press in order to further impugn Casement's reputation and guarantee his conviction. It worked. Casement was convicted and executed—although I believe the result would probably have been the same without the Black Diaries. In the years following, the Black Diaries were considered to be dubious, papery slanders tricked up by perfidious Albion. Then, in 1994, the diaries were released and, it turned out, no, they were true! Casement was a gay man and what were detailed on the pages in his unique handwriting was the substance of his real relationships with other men. For Sebald, the diaries' confirmation of the truth of Casement's nature was a source of joy.

'Casement's homosexuality,' he writes 'sensitized him to the continuing oppression, exploitation, enslavement and destruction, across the borders of social class and race, of those who were furthest from the centres of power.' In other words, if Casement hadn't been the man he was, he wouldn't have done what he did, in Africa, South America, or Ireland. His 'homosexuality', Sebald believes, was not a key but the key.

★

I moved to Northern Ireland with my wife and our children in 1989. We settled outside Enniskillen in County Fermanagh but I got a job as a researcher in a documentary film company in Belfast and, in the week, I stayed in town and lived in an old Georgian house in the city centre owned by the accountant of the company where I worked. His stock was Dublin merchant class, he often told me. He went to Gonzaga and UCD before going to London and Channel Four. He did the Daily Telegraph crossword every day. His Belfast street (which went to the city centre) was used by the IRA to bring their bombs in and to deter them British army patrols passed up and down many times every hour. One evening we worked out how many Land Rovers passed in a year and how much that cost. It was an astronomical sum and as far as I'm concerned it was worth it. Very early one summer's morning, the IRA left a 3500 lb bomb in a transit near our front door: a soldier smashed his way in and yanked my landlord's partner and baby son (he was away in London) and me into the street where we joined our neighbours who had been pulled from their houses by other soldiers. It was a Biblical scene. In our nightclothes we all fled to the Ulster Hall. We were given tea and sandwiches; as dawn broke we heard the controlled explosion, a sickening sound one registered in the gut. When we returned in the morning, not a window in the street remained. I spent the day sweeping glass and negotiating with truculent glaziers.

My job at the film company required reading a lot of books so I could write proposals for programmes. Naturally, I read a lot of Troubles books. One was Martin Dillon's *The Dirty War*. It was a good book but it also meant something personally. Chapter Five 'The Pitchfork Killings' told the story of the brutal murders, on October 23, 1972, of two men, both Catholics, Michael Naan (31, farmer and a civil rights activist) and Andrew Murray (24, farm labourer): Naan and Murray were stabbed to death on a farm in Aghnahinch, a mile south of Newtownbutler. These murders (famous in Fermanagh) were and indeed still are known as the 'pitchfork' murders though no pitchforks were involved, as Dillon says. Naan and Murray were repeatedly stabbed with a 5 ½ inch double-edged knife. In January 1981, more than nine years after the killings, two serving soldiers and one former soldier, all of whom had served in 13 Platoon, D company, 1

Argylls, who were in the Aghnahinch area in October, 1972, pleaded guilty to their roles in the murders of Naan and Murray. Former Platoon Sergeant Stan Hathaway was convicted of two counts of murder and sentenced to life. He was released in 1992. Corporal John Byrne was convicted on one count of murder (the murder of Murray). He got a life sentence too. He was released in 1991. Lance Corporal Ian Chestnut was convicted of manslaughter and was sentenced to four years imprisonment relating to the death of Andrew Murray. Chestnut served less than two years. The officer commanding 13 Platoon in 1972, 2nd Lieutenant Andrew Snowball, pleaded guilty to withholding information and received a sentence of one year, suspended.

I read Dillon's book in the early 1990s, twenty years after the killings and ten after the trial and subsequently I had several conversations about the case with people in Fermanagh. Broadly speaking, opinion was symmetrically sectarian. Those who were not sympathetic to the state, spoke of the convicted NCOs and their officer as cold -blooded murderers. As they had it, the state had executed two innocent men because they were Catholics. Those who, broadly speaking, supported the state, whispered darkly about dire times and Naan's culpability. 1972, was a terrible year, they said. Just look at the calendar before the Naan/Murray murders, they said. March, 1972, Private Johnny Fletcher, murdered Enniskillen. July, part-time UDR soldier, John Johnston, shot in the hand and leg in Wattlebridge, not far from Naan's farm. August 7, Lance Corporal William Creighton, shot dead Magheraveely, near Newtownbutler. August 26, Lance Corporal Alfred Johnston and Private James Eames, killed Enniskillen while inspecting a booby-trapped car. August 28, 57-year-old Protestant farmer William Trotter killed by a booby-trap bomb left on his farm in the townland of Drumralla which was directly opposite Naan's farm. Trotter was not in the UDR. September 3, Private Francis Veitch shot dead outside Kinawley RUC station. September 21, Private Thomas Bullock, UDR, part-timer, and his wife, Emily, shot dead by the IRA at their home at Killynick, just a couple of miles from Naan's farm. The meaning of these killings and the intimidation that went in conjunction with them (the Latimer brothers, for instance, again UDR part-timers who again lived close to Michael Naan, had been driven out of their farm in the autumn too) was obvious. The IRA were ethnically cleansing the area (this was the belief even if that wasn't the language used) and something had to be done. The Argylls, the tough guys who'd put the rebels in Aden in their box, arrived in South Fermanagh on October 21 to do just this. The very next day, October 22, Robin Bell, UDR soldier and farmer, and also a neighbour of Michael Naan, was murdered at his farm. His father and brother who were with him, were lucky to escape alive. The next day, October 23, according to those who felt the army's actions were comprehensible, the Argylls moved against Naan, and his associate, Murray. And why wouldn't they? Naan was a Catholic, a bachelor, reasonably wealthy, a bit cocky, a civil rights activist, a troublemaker, obdurate. Was he in the IRA? Who was to say, they said. Maybe. Given his civil rights activism chances were he was. But even if he wasn't in the movement he was with the movement. He had to be dealt with and dealt with he was.

And what of the trial? I'd always ask next. Didn't it suggest the soldiers had lost the run of themselves, which most definitely wasn't supposed to happen with professional soldiers, which in turn suggested that their officers were negligent. Those with police, army or Loyalist connections, when I said this, rather than engage with my point always simply dismissed the trial as a disgrace; the convicted soldiers, they said, had only done their duty—they'd taken out some bad guys—and then at the trial they'd been thrown to the wolves to please the RCs. Unionists, when I mentioned the trial, conceded the convicted Argylls had overstepped the marked, but added that in a pressure cooker situation that did sometimes happen. Yes, they always continued, two men died but no inference should be drawn about the army overall. They were a disciplined force. Plus, they always ended, there had been a trial. The state had convicted its own. British justice, blind and impartial, had again prevailed and the rotten apples had been removed. I didn't know what to think about this. I knew soldiers went bonkers in riots but how could they lose the plot on a calm autumn evening in South Fermanagh? It didn't make sense. But if the red mist explanation was ruled out, then all I was left with was the sceptical anti-state explanation. Naan and Murray, Irish-born UK citizens, had been brutally murdered by their own country's army. It was terrorism, by the state. Could that really be the case?

In 1991, I started working as a prison teacher. I lent my copy of *The Dirty War* to a prisoner and never got it back. Sometimes, passing Naan's farm, as I did from time to time, I remembered what happened, but that was the height of it. Really I forgot about the murders until Christmas 2020 when I gave someone a lift. She was from Newtownbutler, born and bred and the 'pitchfork' murders, as they were still wrongly called, came up. 'The Brits killed them men because they were Catholics,' my speaker said. 'Simple as. And the ones who went to prison were just the fall guys.'

My interest was re-aroused. I got new copy of Dillon's *The Dirty War*, but it wasn't until two days after the fall of Kabul that I re-read Chapter Five. Then I got on to the internet to do a bit of reading around the subject and pretty quickly—proving once again Edward Snowden is right, 'they're' watching—I was alerted to a book called *An Army of Tribes: British Cohesion, Deviancy and Murder in Northern Ireland* by Edward Burke. I got a copy, from the library not Amazon. Pages 227 to 335 were devoted to Naan and Murray's murders. I read them.

Very clear and chastening they are. Burke's text offers a forensic de-construction of all that is known about the 'pitchfork' murders and relies—and this is revelatory—on the testimonies of the soldiers who were there—the convicted and their peers. The testimonies—the words—of the soldiers, are full of gaps and lacunae, as well as being contradictory and self-serving. No soldier, and this is evident in every word, wants to do more than say the bare minimum. They are all economical with the truth. OK, you might say—why wouldn't they be? Nobody wants to incriminate themselves. I can accept that. But this fidelity to economy with the truth—and this what the testimonies really evidence—is also an article of faith for the RUC, the military police, and the entire criminal justice system. The giving of the bare minimum is not just something the Argylls practised; everyone was at this. Thus, what you understand when you read Burke's narrative is that the investigation which didn't get at the facts was a beautiful and deft collaboration between all the parties with one purpose—to close down a full understanding in order to cement the following: one, three NCOs went rogue and their officer, nice young Lieutenant Snowball, was powerless to stop them; and two, the murders were the aberrant acts of oddballs who were acting independently of the command structure. The trouble with this version, of course, are the testimonies that are supposed to support it. The testimonies are so full of holes if any were a boat that boat would sink like a sieve. The testimonies provide an account, yes, but it's an account that makes no sense. Why the soldiers did what they did to Naan and Murray is impossible to understand from the soldiers' words or the state's case. So, in the absence of an explanation, what might have happened? The most one can say is that it isn't enough to say three NCOs went rogue: they were part of a system with a command structure which had convinced itself Michael Naan was a militant Republican (he wasn't) who had to be dealt with in order to save lives. That command structure sent the soldiers in to do something to Naan—whether just to frighten him or worse isn't clear. Unfortunately for Andrew Murray, he was there too. After Naan was murdered Murray couldn't be left alive; so he was dispatched like his employer. That's the best explanation there is given the little we know. But unless you read *An Army of Tribes*, where you will find a much better account of what probably transpired than I have given, this is not what is generally believed. What is generally believed is what the trial combined with the Argyll and Sutherland Highlander's omertà policy put into the public record. It's the bad apples story, and oh my goodness, how it's taken. Result: the stain of the 'pitchfork' murders—and how telling we still identify these crimes with a weapon that wasn't used, which by the way was a feint deliberately leaked into the public realm in 1972 to cause confusion—has more or less been expunged. Today the crimes are not popularly connected to the Argyll and Sutherland Highlanders like Bloody

Sunday is connected to the Paratroop Regiment. Indeed, if the murders are remembered at all it's as a footnote, or a blip. Today they're half way down the Orwellian memory hole and as they slide from view they're taking the victims, Naan and Murray, down with them.

On a sunny August day with friends I boarded a boat at Killynick. My friends were there for a day out but I was there to get a look at the area where the 'pitchfork' murders occurred as seen from the Erne waterways system that threads through South Fermanagh. We puttered off. The water was brown and still. On either side, lush meadows, screens of trees and fat cattle. We passed Gad Tower (a folly); saw Crom Castle behind trees (a grey, Scottish, baronial building) and then went along the top of Inishfendra island (searched for arms by the Argylls just prior to Naan and Murray's murders, searched perhaps by the very men who killed them) and saw Bloody Pass, where the Jacobite Army, having fled the scene of the battle of Newtownbutler which was fought n 1689 at Aghnahinch, were driven into the Erne by the pursuing Protestant forces. They all were either drowned or piked.

The excursion was going very nicely and then as happens it stopped going nicely. The steering cable snapped. We limped to Crom and moored. Children jumping from the jetty, screaming with joy. A party of ladies under umbrellas, one with a grey Schnauzer standing on her lap. Irish Chekhovian. I stepped ashore, walked about a bit. All of D Company were moved to a camp here at Crom a few hours after Naan and Murray's murders. I wondered if Lieutenant Snowball and his NCOs, Hathaway, Byrne and Chestnut had walked the paths I was walking, or admired the view from the jetty where our boat was moored. In the television film of the murders they would.

I went inside an estate building in search of refreshments. The route to the café went through the Crom Castle museum. The exhibition told an anodyne story of plantation (seventeenth century), expansion (eighteenth century), consolidation (nineteenth century), and survival (twentieth century). The Catholics displaced to make way for the estate were acknowledged but nothing more. There was no sense here of what power had done, but it was ever thus. I can report, however, there was a very impressive stuffed otter.

★

The Americans departed Kabul on 31 August 2021. In the days that followed, on television, interviews with terrified embassy guards and cooks, NGO workers and army interpreters and footage from Kabul's streets showing men with guns and mutilated Afghani women's faces on billboard hoardings and shop fronts alternated with Conservative politicians explaining how none of this was the UK's fault. From the get go it was obvious— there would be no coming clean, no honesty, just the approved story: the UK by 'being' in Afghanistan had protected Britain for two decades by preventing Islamic terrorists from putting down roots in Afghan soil and simultaneously had improved Afghan lives a little, until the Yanks ratted on us that is. As I listened, I found myself thinking about the 1981 trial of those accused of Naan and Murray's murders that did not establish the truth but did limit the roster of culprits to three NCOs and a junior officer, because there in microcosm was what I was experiencing in macrocosm now in regard to Afghanistan. In 2021, just as in 1981, no one would be held to account for the Afghan calamity. No one senior at any rate. Some things never changed, it seemed.

For defence against these dark thoughts during September's early mild days, I re-read Sebald's chapter on Casement and Conrad and encountered, once again, the lovely Sebaldian premise that Casement's hot molten core—his sexuality—was the source of his principle, the motor of everything. I found myself agreeing and it made such sweet sense—the sort one craves in difficult times: only when you locate the magma, the real you deep within, will you or can you speak truth to power. In your pith lies your salvation.

Post Script: After completing this essay, Roger Casement's statue went up in Dún Laoghaire. The sage's time has come, perhaps?

Lighthouse Keeping
Gail McConnell

'Lighthouse Keeping'

Seas pleat
winds keen
fogs deepen
ships lean no
doubt, and
the lighthouse
keeper keeps
a light for
those left out.
It is intimate
and remote both
for the keeper
and those afloat.

This favourite poem of mine, by the American poet Kay Ryan, is on my mind again. A storm. Rough winds.

Deep fog. Wild seas. And a bright beam in the darkness. A house on the horizon. 'A light for those left out'. A light which travels between land and sea. Between the keeper and the sailor. A light which connects, for a time. Come the dawn, out with the light. Come the darkness, out comes the light. Now you see me. Now you don't. But when you need it most, in the wildness, the terror, the midnight hours, out it shines.

It is intimate
and remote both
for the keeper
and those afloat.

The poem was with me in the dark of a gallery in Belfast a few weeks back, on the opening night of an exhibition called 'Lighthouse' by the photographer Donovan Wylie. Like me, Wylie was born in Belfast. I've admired his work for some time, and *Maze*, his book of photographs of the Maze prison, was particularly influential on a recent book of mine, *The Sun is Open*. My father was assistant governor in the Maze and was murdered by the IRA outside our home in Belfast in 1984. I was three-and-a-half. Donovan Wylie's photographs of that place my father knew so well, let me see something of what he must have seen daily, or perhaps stopped noticing: the prison's strange elements and zones—Inertias, Steriles, H-blocks, Yards, Sports Fields, Cells, Ablutions, Chapel, The Void.

I wrote to Donovan to thank him for his work and ask for his address to send him a book and he invited me to the opening night of this new exhibition. Immediately after the Brexit referendum of June 2016, Donovan began to photograph lighthouses on these islands and in France, as a way of processing some of the complexities of identity, insularity and isolationism.

I walk around the exhibition with my friend Tim, a painter and photographer. We stand and look. And look. It is hard to look away. These are huge photographs, printed on thin sheets of paper and pinned to the wall. Black and white is the wrong phrase for the palette used. There are so many tones of grey, silver, ash. Each is uniquely lit—with multiple lights, spotlighting and shadowing these—well, what are they? Landscapes? Seascapes? Both? Whatever they are, they are painterly. The tiny pixels conspire in painterly textures—sea and sky, water and cloud: undulation, ripple, wave, wrinkle, swell, billow. Here, the windswept sea is a desert. And here the endless stretch of land is a tide line. And in each photograph:

> the lighthouse
> keeper keeps
> a light for
> those left out.

A pinprick. A punctum. A beacon. A tear in the paper. We look and look and look. And see the light. Which is the afterglow of a distant lighthouse. As far away, Donovan tells us, as 16-25 miles away.

It seems timeless. And yet already it has been extinguished. Relit. Extinguished. Relit. Such is its pattern of existence.

In one photograph, we cannot see the light. This absence unnerves me. I need to believe it is there. But what is this light a lighthouse casts out?

It's a warning sign. Boats beware. Land ahoy. Dangerous rocks up ahead.

It's a welcome sign. Boats come moor. Harbour ahoy. Warmth and shelter ahead.

But even a warning sign is a welcome sign. Better to know the danger to navigate the risk. We need this light. This is the feeling Wylie's 'Lighthouse' prompts. We need this light. And never more so than as new borders are assembled, new restrictions imposed. Never more so than through divorce and separation. Never more so than through bad politics, neglect and negligence. Never more so than through loneliness and displacement.

The sea distances us and draws us close. It makes Ireland an island. And it makes us part of a network in an archipelago, a group of islands connected by waterways. Little wonder a sea border has grown so contentious. We're in one of two centenaries this year, depending on your politics: the partition of Ireland or the beginning of Northern Ireland. It's a death or a birth. Or something of both. And now Brexit, a global pandemic, an immigration crisis and a climate emergency has made many of us feel even more insecure. Even more at sea.

Warning sign. Welcome sign. We need this light.

My thoughts turn to another lighthouse—wished for, wanted and imagined. The one created by Virginia Woolf, in her great masterpiece: *To the Lighthouse*, published in 1927. In the novel, the artist Lily Briscoe is turning over in her mind 'all the things she could not say':

> Was there no safety? No learning by heart of the ways of the world? No guide, no shelter, but all was miracle, and leaping from the pinnacle of a tower into the air? Could it be.... that this was life?— startling, unexpected, unknown?

Preparing to give a lecture on the novel, I turn to Woolf's essay on 'The Cinema', published the previous year, where she writes:

> All is hubble-bubble, swarm and chaos. We are peering over the edge of a cauldron in which fragments of all shapes and savours seem to simmer; now and again some vast form heaves itself up and seems about to haul itself out of chaos.

Hubble-bubble, swarm and chaos. It's a terrifying vision of modernity. And what is this 'vast form', heaving itself up from the chaos? My thoughts turn to W.B. Yeats and his great poem, 'The Second Coming':

When a vast image out of *Spiritus Mundi*
Troubles my sight: somewhere in sands of the desert
A shape with lion body and the head of a man,
A gaze blank and pitiless as the sun,
Is moving its slow thighs, while all about it
Reel shadows of the indignant desert birds.

'Things fall apart; the centre cannot hold.'
'All is hubble-bubble, swarm and chaos.'
We need this light. Through the darkness. Through the deep.

But when we cannot see or sense it, how do we go on? Extinguished. Relit. Extinguished. Relit. How do we make our way without this beckoning, this beacon of light?

A favourite sentence, from Beckett's *Worstward Ho*: 'Plod on, and never recede'. But how, when 'all is hubble-bubble, swarm and chaos'?

Creatures have taught me how to go on. The narwhal. The octopus. The cuttlefish. The worm. Creatures who live in the darkness and the deep. Creatures who have devised strategies of survival. Ways to live, and even to thrive, in places where living seems almost impossible.

Our toddler has a blue plastic narwhal with a long grey tusk. He dives it into the bathwater—splash!—tusk first, body following after. It's an amazing thing, that tusk, or tooth. Home to 10 million little tubules, its sensory capabilities let the narwhal detect changes in the ocean's salt concentration and then steer clear of sea ice cover, swimming instead towards the breathing holes it needs to survive. Known as the unicorn of the sea, the narwhal taught me something about living in dangerous waters and difficult times. And so I wrote this poem:

Narwhal

(1)

This living under glass is all he knows.
Or living with its threat—
the encroachment
of ice. In Arctic waters
the corpse whale roams.

The fear of suffocation
drives echolocation.

The echo after pulse
confirms/ denies
the dot dot dash dot wish
to live with news of air holes
or their lack.

That horn which is not horn
but tooth, biologists misread.

Jousting lance, they said, his tusk
which seemed less tusk than sword—
a nine-foot spiral-structured blade.

Perforated to perfection, it's a survival aid.
Our bare life prompts invention.

(2)

The beast receives and reads the sea
that purls into each cavity.
He knows where icebergs melt
and form
by measuring salinity.

Any loss of sensitivity
is deathly here, he knows,
though the ocean spreads below,
the ice above, on on it goes—the capture
and release of water in the hollows.

The problem is the cure—
the scouring and discharging sea.

Salt accrues in apertures—
the price of intimacy.

Reading that poem again, I hear something of Kay Ryan's lighthouse in the final lines. Intimate and remote. The sea rushes in to fill the tiny cavities inside the narwhal's tusk. And rushes out again, flowing back into the waters. But in leaving the tusk, they also leave a trace: salt. Which gathers and accrues. Over time, the salt's presence will diminish the tusk's powers of sensitivity. Being intimate with one's home place—the sea—comes with a cost. The cavities clog. Sensing salinity, and safety, grows more difficult. Not impossible. But difficult.

Living in the long aftermath of my father's murder, and living as a quote unquote 'public victim' of the quote unquote 'Troubles', I know these depths. I know this darkness. I know the fear of suffocation. And the rising panic that this time, the airholes are just beyond reach. Being sensitive to his environment ensures the narwhal's survival. But that sensitivity means being in touch with the threat of death.

And still, 'on on it goes'. For what else can this creature do, but make a way where it seems impossible? Swimming through icy waters until the narwhal finds a place to breathe.

Down there in the depths, the octopus makes her way. If attacked and entangled by a predator, she performs a magical act: an act of adaptation, escape and self-preservation. She self-severs the entangled limb and simply swims away. She lets go a part of herself to stay alive.

Octopus

I

With no internal shell you keep
yourself together in a sac
& the matter of attachment.

All you know you know by touch; shape,
texture and scale you draw into
the mouth of every flowering cup.

From pit to tip the suckers spring.
Each flicker of skin criss-crossing
your path a chance to make contact,

a chance to draw a body not
your own into your care, or spread
out into theirs. The emptiness

you know you've laboured to transpose.
Your vacuum sets their course, carries
these objects of desire towards

your hearts so that they hold; hemmed in
in eight soft limbs & the borders
of concavities, folded fast.

The things that cling can't always be
predicted—slivers of mirror,
bits of bone, curls, keys, a toy gun.

Attachment: is it grace or grasp?
All things unknown familiar in
the peeling off and letting go.

II

Panicked, with inky melanin
you make a slipstream to get free
or make autotomy an art

rewriting your anatomy.
Camouflage has failed, mimicry
cannot hold off attack. Scoring

your arms with incisions those claws.
Whose cuts are these? Who bruises, chews
at your skin, initiates this

severing? You watch it detach,
float away from you. Coppered blood
infuses the already blue.

Self-sabotage, the first and last

stage of collage, the cutting up
without the glue. The bitten limb

goes unattached, but is renewed.
You didn't know you knew the art
of self-repair until alone

those hundred days, watching something
grow. New cups bloom the length of you;
mouths opening by small degrees.

The whipping fins can be withstood,
the gripping jaws. All that issues
from the deep, in all likelihood.

I loved standing with our toddler at our local aquarium, watching an octopus coil and twist behind the glass, and watching his face—amazed by this limby creature. The octopus knows that loss is survivable. Let your limb go, and still you go on—more vulnerable, a bit wonky, but on you go, making your way. And, in time, something new comes. Slowly, slowly. Small degrees. Something new comes, and still you are forever changed by loss. Now all your movements bear this out. It's in your gait, behind your eyes, and shadowing your gestures. You sense that here, in this place—where we're living after, with or through trauma. And everything it brings. 'All that issues / from the deep.'

At the end of 2021 I was spent. I'd been giving readings from *The Sun Is Open* at festivals and events, and doing loads of interviews for radio and podcasts, while teaching and supervising and doing other bits of research and writing. Then I got Covid. Then our toddler got Covid. I was ready to collapse. I wanted to collapse. Talking about the book had taken it out of me. I had created an expansive book that moves between child and adult voices to give you the event of my father's murder and its long aftermath for me, and a 1980s Belfast childhood, watching SuperTed and Bananaman, playing Tetris on my Gameboy, and going to Sunday School and summer camps. I worked on my own to make this book. Quietly, privately, at my own pace. But then the book was in the world and the next challenge was to embody the work: voice it; breathe the poems into the world. And after months of that, I needed to curl up in a ball. Or to sever a limb and swim away.

Loss is painful. For the octopus, bloody. But if there is an art of self-repair, it can only be discovered through loss. In her wonderful villanelle, 'One Art', Elizabeth Bishop initiates 'the art of losing'. And, to my mind, the octopus does the same.

Closer to home, and closer to the surface, there's another creature whose patterns of behaviour are no mere means of survival—but of flourishing. The earthworm. A creature I admire, perhaps most of all.

Worm

Burrowing in your allotted patch you
 move through the dark, muscles contracting one by one

in every part, lengthening and shortening
 the slick segmented tube of you, furrows in your wake.

Devising passages for water, air,
 you plot the gaps that keep the structure from collapse.

Dead things you know. Plants and creatures both.
 Your grooves shift matter, sifting as you go.

Eyeless, your appetite aerates.
 Eating the world, you open it.

You ingest to differentiate.
 Under the foot-stamped earth, you eat into a clot

of leaf mould, clay and mildew, and express what you can
 part with, as self-possessed as when you started.

Your secretions bind the soil,
 your shit enriches it. How things lie

now will be undone, will reoccur. You, a surface-level

archivist

sensing all there is

can be gone through. The body borne
within its plot.

The worm, seeing nothing, senses all there is. It makes
a way, eating and shitting, eating and shitting, and as
it goes, it fertilises the soil and enables the flourishing
of plant life—flowers and fruit and food. Everything
changes. Everything recurs. And on the worm goes. This
is a creature whose way of living says to me: wherever
your plot, whatever your lot, however much death is
around you, live as best you can, and trust that all can
be borne. It's a simple life, eating and excreting, and a
repetitive one. But what comes of it is extraordinary: soil
aerated, drained, fertilised, so that everything that grows
can thrive.

'furrows in your wake.' Tide lines. Beams of light.
The beacon in the tower turns and turns again. The
lighthouse casts its ray across the surface of the water,
home to the narwhal and the octopus, and across the
rugged headland of Torr Head, where the worm writhes
the soil. 'A light for / those left out.'

We stand with Donovan Wylie in the last small
chamber of the gallery, where four final photographs
hang north, south, east and west. We've been wandering
through the exhibition for a second time, this time in

his company, as he describes making the photographs, in the ten-minute window of time that opens the moment the lighthouse is lit and closes the moment city lights appear. Like me, he loves Woolf's novel, and we talk of its lighthouse and Woolf's vision. We talk of parenting and motorbikes and Hiroshi Sugimoto. We talk of parents and parents dying and the living that happens after. We talk of chance encounters and faith and calculations. We talk of these lighthouses and the difficult times we're in.

We need this light. We pivot, toe and heel, away from the lighthouse in the north. We pivot to the east, and back. And then to the south, and back. And lastly to the west, and back. And do it all again. Pivoting within the small chamber of this last dark room, turning and turning to the other lighthouse, to these sources of light that surround us on all sides. Intimate and remote. Both for the keeper and those afloat.

And then we're out. Into the bright light of the vestibule. Into the orange of the sodium street lights. Into the candlelight of the pub's corner snug. Into another week. And another. And another. With lighthouses on the mind and in view. The punctum. The pinprick. The beacon. The tear in the paper. We carry it with us. Though the wind screeches. Though the fog deepens. Though the tide rises. This light, we keep it close.

A Place Between
Henrietta McKervey

I don't know where he is. My father. I mean, I know
his current location: an incongruously flashy urn on a
shelf in the two-room standalone he had built to replace
the garage. With no apparent irony (though it could be
hard to tell), he always called this building the sunroom,
despite it having the temperature of a butcher's cold store
on all but the hottest days.

I've only ever seen his urn once, so five minutes ago, I
nipped out for a second look. It's black and marbled with
greenish-gold veins, like a tabletop in a casino. He had a
fondness for cheap casinos, yet this design doesn't seem to
be quite him. Taking inspiration from gravestones rather
than fabrics strikes me as a missed opportunity for urn
manufacturers. His personality would be better suited to
a natty pinstripe; deepest black shot through with grey
and topped with a snowy slick of white. A suit worn with
a perfectly pressed shirt.

I'm looking for my father because I want to find where
he is today, in my life. And more than that, where he is
now within his own. Occasionally, on a bright winter's

morning, one of those cheering days where the sun gifts rainbows to the wet street, I think I see him. A tall, broad figure striding ahead, wearing a navy overcoat, burgundy trousers, and a Greek fisherman's cap. Always rounding the corner, always just moving out of sight. Lots of older men dress like that, I tell myself, rolling my eyes at the colour of the trousers.

I won't find him where I live in Dublin, but I might find him in his house. Which is why I'm sitting alone at my parents' dining table in Belfast, looking at photos, looking through his things, playing a quiet, solitary game of hunt-the-dad.

My mother walks into the room, mobile in hand. I've just had a WhatsApp from Anne, she says. She's in Ederney. She reads the rest of my cousin's message aloud: *Suspected cannabis factory worth six hundred thousand pounds discovered in Fermanagh - in Ederney.* Wow, I say. My mother gently taps her finger against the screen as she counts Anne's exclamation marks. Ten! she tallies. Wow, I say again, fully on board with this level of excitement. *In Ederney!* we chorus, and I know we are both immediately picturing my father's home place, a village that has always struck me not so much as sleepy as unconscious. Despite knowing that its five hundred inhabitants aren't all related to us, I've always assumed they kind-of are really, so we immediately begin joking about who might be involved. A McKervey cartel, my mother laughs. Imagine!

After my father's sudden death in June 2017, people

came in and out of the house all day. Early in the evening of the second day—Sunday—a large car pulled up in the driveway. Cousins, an uncle and aunt, a friend of the uncle, a cousin's girlfriend, and a kindly randomer whose exact connection I never quite figured out but who had an anecdote about dropping coal to my father when he was a student, all tumbled out. I stood at the front door and watched. For a second, I forgot why they were here, and turned around to call Dad to come see the clown car. It took a few minutes before everyone was arranged onto seats hastily grabbed from other rooms, and supplied with drinks and plates of the food that kind-hearted Anne (*you'll need sandwiches!!!!!*) had filled the fridge with earlier in the afternoon.

My mother began to explain what had happened on the Friday evening. How my father had been frying two steaks, how he suddenly said he felt dizzy, how he fell to the floor. How he spoke only one more sentence. How he died hours later. I leaned over to Uncle John, my father's youngest brother, sitting in Dad's favourite chair. Uncle John? I whispered, comforted not just by his presence, but by how remarkably alike my godfather and father were. Aye, Henrietta? he said, leaning forward too. Uncle John, who's minding Ederney while you're all here? Don't worry, he said. Sure, didn't we leave all the lights on?

Now that I'm writing the name, I realise how little I know about my father's home place. I google Ederney (the cannabis bust—in which no McKerveys turn out to have been involved—seriously skews the results). Its Irish name, Eadarnaidh, means *middle place* or *place between*. That's about right, I think. In my life, it is somewhere defined by where it's not: it's where my father lived then left, first to boarding school in Armagh, then university in Belfast, and then on and on, other cities, other countries, but never another village.

When I was a kid, I enjoyed our rare visits to Ederney. Uncle John would stride out from behind the counter of his bathroom supplies shop and take my two brothers and me to the local newsagent and buy us more sweets than we'd seen in a year. Or if he was busy with a customer, he'd give me a fiver and send me off, trusting me to do the job myself (I never let him down). He wore a white coat over his clothes, like a doctor. I liked that our surname was written above the biggest shops on the main street: J McKervey & Sons builders' providers and bathroom supplies on one side, a vast tile showroom on the other. But the thing I used to enjoy most was watching my father being interrogated by his brothers and sisters. He was a man who didn't believe in answering a question if he felt it didn't warrant a response. He was never rude— in fact he was a very polite person, but reserve can be an intimidating quality, and it often made people quieter, nervier, around him. Less sure of themselves, as though he was an unpredictable horse, liable to buck. But with his siblings (he was third-youngest of eight; five boys, three girls) he had no escape. Using his own name as a spear, they would ask question after question, each one beginning *Tony, what do you...* and hopping between parish and politics, living neighbours and dead relations. As I got older, I went from being an impressed child (he must really be something that they need to know what he thinks!) to a sceptical teenager (what are they asking him for? He doesn't have a clue) to an amused adult (I bet he's hating so many questions!). Now I see these exchanges for what they were: sincere regard and respect on both sides.

I know if I go to Ederney I will find people who loved him, but not him.

I walk upstairs and look for him here, in his wardrobe. A fine layer of dust dandruffs the shoulders of his suits. I count twelve pairs of trousers, six suits, three summer jackets, five shirts on hangers. Fewer than the last time I looked; the hangers are now loosely grouped in the middle of the rails. My mother has recently begun to find new homes for his clothes. She gave me the only possession of his I asked for: a navy Aran jumper which she made and he wore often. I never once heard him describe an item of clothing in terms she or I use—*lovely, adore, happy*—but regular wear speaks its own vocabulary of approval.

The best place to look for him is in his work. He was a research scientist. It was his being, not his employment. He was a Professor of Organic Chemistry who founded the Business Unit of Almac Sciences (more of this anon). He won awards, wrote hundreds of research papers, invented things, taught thousands of students. We lived in Cork for thirteen years while he worked at UCC, though he returned to Queen's again in 1990 to head up the Research Division in the School of Chemistry. A friend of mine who had been in his first-year class at UCC said he was nicknamed 'the typewriter' because during lectures he would walk from one side of the room to the other, across and back, a sentence at a time.

In January 2018, a memorial seminar is organised in his honour at UCC. My mum and I go. He used to walk into the lab in the mornings and ask *what's new?* one of his favourite PhD students tells me. And he didn't mean had you seen anything good on TV, or how did the hurling go. He only wanted to hear what had happened in your work since the last time he had asked. I laugh. In the year before he died, he used to *what's new?* me on the phone every Friday morning. At the seminar there are presentations about chemistry, which I don't understand, and people talking about him, which I enjoy.

And then a very lovely thing happens.

The organiser, Anita, gestures to my mother to come up to the podium. As the previous speaker was concluding, I noticed the tip of my mother's index finger running busily over her thumbnail. This is something she has always done: composing lists or notes on her nail, or maybe simply to help order her thoughts. I've never asked. Her finger has been moving madly for a couple of minutes, a miniature Ouija board gone crazy. I am nervous of her getting up to speak. I'm not concerned about what she might say, she has the ease and grace to charm any room, but she has been unwell, and the long car journey from Belfast to Cork followed by a day of sitting, standing, walking has been hard on her. She looks tired. She stands at the lectern and takes a breath.

Northern Ireland used to be such a little place, she says. She moved there from America in 1967 (she is Irish, she left Dublin for Chicago in the early 1960s and worked in a department store before training as an air hostess and moving to Boston, where she and my father met). She wondered what on earth she had done leaving Boston for Belfast; what mistake had she made. The people were kind, she says, but still. Sometimes people aren't enough. And then she begins to talk about three men from Northern Ireland, each of whom made the place something special. Different. Each of whom left it better—more confident, assured, stable—than they found it.

These three, she says, three contemporaries, were Tony McKervey, Allen McClay and Seamus Heaney. Fermanagh, Tyrone, Derry. (I don't know if Allen McClay, who died in 2010 and Seamus Heaney, who died in 2013, ever met, but my father and Seamus were friends at Queen's decades earlier when both wrote poetry for a college magazine. I think we know which of the two that worked out best for. At the time, Seamus was the only one with a car; he would collect Dad and his pal John from their digs on a Saturday night and drive into town, the lads sitting in the back, thinking they were the bee's knees.) She describes how Allen and my father met in the 1990s, when Galen, Allen's first pharmaceutical company—and Northern Ireland's first ever one-billion-pound company—bought Qu-Chem, the Queen's campus start-up my father and his friend Brian Walker had established. Allen went on to be one of the biggest benefactors in the university's history. The McClay Library at Queen's—which was officially opened by Seamus Heaney, a neat touch—is named for him. Allen was a kind, quick-witted man who drove such a banger of a car that he used to joke it doubled in value whenever he filled the tank. My mother quotes Allen's story of his retirement in 2002: *I retired on the Friday, and by the Monday I'd had enough and decided to go back to work.* Going 'back to work' for him meant founding Almac, a life sciences company dedicated to advancing human health, with my father, who was younger and still some years shy of his first retirement, as technical director.

My mother explains how these three men, through literature, science and entrepreneurship, altered the present and the future for the North. How each of their achievements showed how we could feel differently about our own worth. Could have faith in history, pride in ability. All three are dead now, she says, and intertwined. Each in a different way created something permanent but not fixed. Each left a legacy that is deep-rooted yet simultaneously all potential, waiting to be realised.

That was brilliant, I whisper, when she sits down.

A couple of months later (this is the 'anon' I mentioned earlier) she and I go to the Almac offices in Craigavon for lunch and a tour of the building. I haven't been here for years, not since its official opening more than a decade earlier. The chief executive has a surprise for us: they are commemorating my father with a new *Almac McKervey Award for Excellence in Organic Chemistry*, to be given annually to a student. There will be a plaque mounted on the wall in the chemistry building in Queen's to commemorate it, they tell us. A stone fixed to a stone.

Almac has six thousand employees worldwide now. I remember Dad talking about this rapid expansion, and how he decided to give up his large, bright office for a smaller one when space first became tight. When he sort-of-retired, he downsized again, moving to a small room with a glass wall that faced onto a larger, open-plan workspace. After lunch, our guided tour of the building pauses here, my father's last home from home. A man sitting at the desk looks up at the six people—three of whom are his bosses—who have unexpectedly crammed themselves into his office. He is wearing an outdoor jacket and has a computer bag next to him on the desk as though he's just passing through. He looks startled. He's new, he says; he never met Tony. One of my father's former colleagues has been reminiscing about how if he ever had a technical problem he'd seek Tony out, and they'd walk around the lab, discussing it. We'd always end up back here, at the whiteboard, he explains. And

Tony would pause, and then write the solution. And he was always right, he says; the answer would be there. Six heads turn and look at the wall, eager to see the final chemistry problem my father solved. The whiteboard is clear, clean as fresh snowfall. The man behind the desk looks terrified. I'm so sorry, he says: I wiped it only last week.

I move from the dining table across the room, to his desk. His computer is long gone, returned to Almac. A 2017 diary is next to the small pot he stored pens in. His two fountain pens have dried up. I flick through the diary, looking for records of appointments. I leaf through the pages, prepared for the poignancy of a hard stop on June 24th, but it's unused. I can't decide if that is better or worse.

I go outside, and stand at the gate. Osborne Park is a lovely street, leafy and quiet. My mum lives in the semi-detached house they moved to thirty years ago when they returned to Belfast from Cork. It's small in relation to the neighbouring houses, and a doll's house by comparison with some of the vast Victorian villas at the Malone Road end of the street. Across the road is the house I was born into, which we left when I was five—and having spent a year of that time living in a flat in Cambridge, my memories of this house are few and overly-informed by photographs. I do recall the day we moved out though, and Dad telling me to say goodbye to the house, that I'd be going home somewhere new after school. There was a tiny flurry of snow on the ground that morning, and as we walked away he held my hand, in case I'd slip.

I'm not looking for Stolpersteine; he was a man who lived until he was seventy-eight. He was not lost, nor he is forgotten. Perhaps it's a corollary of stumbling stones; his name is already commemorated. I know that from the numbers of people who contacted us after he died. People from all over the world who each had their own version of him, who knew a different man from the one I did.

When we lived in Cork, he had many PhD students from abroad. Nepal and Thailand particularly. I don't know why and even as a child I used to wonder what it was like for them to travel all that distance—many of them going home once a year at most—to Ireland, but of all places in Ireland, to Cork. One man from Thailand, whose name my mum and I can't remember but wish we could, developed a truly impressive Cork accent. Every Christmas Day, Dad and I would collect them one by one from their digs and bring them to our house for dinner.

My father, as I say, was cooking when he collapsed. His last words were *turn the heat off*. He understood the power of detail. He was intricate, precise. Even as he was losing consciousness his instinct was to ensure that the activity was concluded safely. I suppose there is no other way to be in science.

It's getting late. I wander into the kitchen. The heating timer beside the back door has just clicked on. I stand at the sink and look out, at the path leading from the kitchen door to the sunroom. Tall trees at the bottom of the garden sway soundlessly in the wind, black shapes against an inky sky finely streaked with pink. Lights from the house the next street over appear and disappear through the dancing gaps between branches.

I hear my mother moving about upstairs. It's the type of noise I know she misses; the sound of someone else in the house, living their day. He is here, in her heart. In mine.

The windows of the sunroom are dark.

Lapsed
Jan Carson

In 1839, the celebrated architect Sir Charles Lanyon planted over 1500 Scots pines along the edge of what is now the A26 or, as we Ballymena-born folk call it, the Ballymoney Line. Lanyon hoped the roots would extend beneath the road's surface preventing it from subsiding into the boggy peat. The pines flourished. By the time I arrived on the scene, almost a century and a half later, they'd formed a long, leafy tunnel: spindly trunks inclined at a sixty-degree angle, broccoli-green canopy bustling high above the cars and caravans on their way to the coast. In strong wind the trees swayed hypnotically. Like dancing ladies or end-of-night drunks. Some people thought they were haunted. This particular stretch of the road was infamous for bad car accidents. Black ice. Collisions. Drivers falling asleep behind the wheel. People liked to speculate it had something to do with Lanyon's pines.

As a child, I was captivated by the Frosses. It was like entering another underwater world—strange and woozy—to be driven through that dappled light. Like all children raised in this neck of the woods, I knew to draw breath upon sight of the first bent pine and hold that breath, red-faced and panicking, until the final tree appeared in Dad's windscreen. Nobody taught me to do this. It was bred into all the local weans. Back then roads passed for cheap entertainment. My brother and I would beg our parents to take us for a Sunday run to the 'big hill' outside Randalstown (which felt like a rollercoaster if you drove down it fast), or up the 'bumpy road' (whose potholes wreaked havoc on Dad's tyres while we bounced, giddy and seat-belt-free, around the backseat). The Frosses loomed large in my psychogeography. I liked the way it demanded much of me. I liked the leafy, liminal feel of it. And the Gospel signs pinned to every other trunk? Well, I liked the way they terrified me.

I was a sheltered child, raised conservative, rural and Presbyterian. I had a healthy fear of the Second Coming. It often kept me up at night wondering if I was properly saved and why I was not excited about the Lord Jesus Christ's imminent return (this was something our congregation continually prayed for). Each time I came across an 'eternity where?' sign pinned to a tree or painted on a barn—as was the fashion in 1980s Ulster—I'd get a little rush of adrenaline. A jolt of fear so sharp and deep it both terrified and thrilled me. God was talking directly to me. 'Repent or perish,' he was saying. 'Choose you this day who you will follow. For the wages of sin are death.' Driving the length of the Frosses was like an extended—if somewhat shouty—conversation with God himself. The Born Again contingent had a soul-searching quandary pinned to every other tree. I'd hold my breath, consider my eternal destiny and hope—God-willing—to make it out the other end of the tunnel, to Logan's Fashions and the Ballycastle junction beyond.

In early 2015 the majority of the trees at the Frosses were removed, making way for a seven-kilometre extension of the A26. Only 104 of Lanyon's original trees now remain. As far as I can see none of the Gospel signs have survived the cull. This is hardly surprising. The religious landscape of Northern Ireland has changed dramatically since the 80s. Protestants are no longer quite so hell bent on proselytizing. A great number have lost faith in the established church. Some might call them backsliders. Others, people who've finally seen sense and liberated themselves from the stranglehold of Irish religiosity. In his recent book, *The Rise and Fall of Christian Ireland*, Crawford Gribben writes: 'The Irish experience of secularization was sudden, shocking and decisive. On both sides of the border, the tipping point may have occurred in the mid-1990s. In the North, the peace process led to sustained efforts to depoliticize religious identity, as weekly church attendance declined from over 60 percent in 1968 to just over 40 percent in 2004.'

I can't speak for Catholicism in the North, though recent news suggests the influence of the Catholic Church is on a rapidly declining trajectory. In the evangelical

Protestant circles in which I grew up, a similar decline is glaringly apparent. Church attendance is shrinking and congregations aging rapidly, some are even shutting up shop. Church buildings are now repurposed as restaurants, furniture stores, theatres and quirky renovated homes for the *Grand Design* set. There are dwindling numbers of children enrolled in para-church organisations like the Girls' and Boys' Brigades, fewer tent missions, evangelistic campaigns and of course, an obvious lack of roadside reminders to 'turn or burn'. A few remain: archaic relics from a tighter time. There's the text at the end of Portstewart prom, the big stone with the painted verse near Mount Stewart, and that barn you pass on the drive to Bellaghy. (I've always been impressed by its size and audacity.) However, it's now entirely possible to take a run up the coast or down to the Mournes and not once find yourself reminded—in six-foot-high faux Gothic font—that you're also on a highway to Hell.

I had a Northern Presbyterian upbringing. Conservative. Strict. Yet not without love nor a deep sense of belonging. There was tremendous security to be found in this. I was born in Ballymena in 1980. My childhood played out against a background of conflict. I turned eighteen the year we 'got peace'. My specific generation grew up straddling societal change: not just an evolution in the political landscape of the North but also a great tidal shift in the status and influence of the Church. The reasons behind this shift are myriad: a deep suspicion of church collusion with politics, secularization, a slightly—only slightly—more nuanced notion of women's rights, migration and tourism (of both the home and away variety), the impact of other cultures and religions upon the North. Whole books have been written on this topic. I anticipate further books and other artistic interrogations of how evangelical Protestantism has both shaped and destroyed the place I call home. The last few decades have seen artists and thinkers widely critique the Catholic Church. The established Protestant Churches seem to have got away lightly in comparison. Lately, I've felt drawn to explore—both celebrating and critiquing— my own experience of evangelical Protestantism. I have attempted to do this from a moderate position as a one-time member and critical friend of this community.

Growing up in the 80s and early 90s, the Church still formed the bedrock of Ballymena. Evangelical Protestants who served on the local council were fighting the Sunday trading laws, attempting to curb the contemporary craze for line dancing and, most famously, ensuring the— supposedly Satanic—band ELO were not permitted to perform in the Showgrounds. My hometown was the Bible Belt of Ulster. Almost everyone I knew attended Sunday School and at least one other church-based programme: Girls' Brigade, Guides, Youth Club, Christian Endeavour, Good News Club or Campaigners. The Church offered an almost infinite number of free childcare options for parents looking an evening off. Many of these parents were nominal believers. Save for weddings, funerals and baptisms, they never darkened the door of a church. Yet they still held a kind of grudging respect for the Church institution and the basic tenets of Protestant faith. They wished their children to grow up in the same churched manner in which they'd been raised.

My extended family were not nominal. They were believers in the truest sense. Preachers, teachers, ministers and missionaries, I came from a long line of fervently evangelical Protestants. I was saved at four and sitting through hour-long adult sermons by the age of eight. I regularly hosted Gospel meetings with my teddies. I was savvy enough to understand I could sing choruses or hand out the hymn books but preaching—even to stuffed animals—was a role reserved for my brother or male cousin. The church community was everything. Our family attended services four times on Sunday and at least four more times throughout the week. In the summer we attended Christian holiday camps and Bible schools. We socialised with other families in our congregation and, though we were praying for their salvation, kept unbelieving friends at a careful distance. As the Bible dictated, we were to be in the world but not influenced by it.

My churched childhood marked me both physically and emotionally. For years I sported a burn on my right shin where my bare leg had made fidgety contact with the heating pipe which ran the length of our family pew. Psychologically, the marks lasted longer. Though I'm no longer adhering to the strict religious doctrines of my youth, I've struggled to shake off the constraints of fundamentalist legalism. I still can't dance. While I no longer believe the impulse is sinful, I can't seem to convince my limbs of this truth. I struggle to lose control in any sense; loss of control was equated with wantonness and, ultimately, sin. I also remain a martyr to chronic do-goodery. The doctrine of placing others' needs before my own was drummed into me at a very impressionable age.

In my thirties I lost my faith, then slowly pieced it back together only to find it no longer resembled the way of life I'd previously known. I could not reconcile the tight, conservative teachings of the Church in which I'd grown up, with the world I'd encountered once I ventured outside. Hannah Adger, the child protagonist of my novel *The Raptures*, journeys through a similar period of deconstruction. After an otherworldly encounter she finds herself in church thinking 'maybe everything's more complicated than she thought... The roof is peeling off Hannah's brain. This morning the church feels very small.' The loss or re-imagining of faith can be an excruciating experience. It was for me. It was the hardest, loneliest experience I've ever been through. So many of the questions I felt compelled to ask and the seismic shifts in my thinking cut right to the bones of who I was. And am. And wish to be.

In their book *Evangelical Journeys*, Claire Mitchell

and Gladys Ganiel explain how Northern Irish evangelicalism—where the church often exists as family, social life and moral compass—is structured to make leaving, or even transforming religious belief, a 'bittersweet process'. Many so-called 'backsliders' like me 'acknowledged a range of feelings of vulnerability and isolation early on in the process.' To leave behind everything you've known and relearn the world can— and I say this with some degree of irony—feel a lot like a second birth. Sometimes, I'm still angry about living so long beneath the oppressive hand of Northern Irish evangelicalism. I'm sad for the experiences I missed out on as a child and teenager. Sad also for the friendships which have become lost or strained since moving away from this community. I am ashamed of the bigoted views and practices to which I once subscribed. However, at times, I also find myself nostalgic for my Presbyterian past. Back then I felt such a strong sense of belonging, and consequently I felt safe and secure. If I'm honest, part of me also misses the restrictions and rules which, whilst difficult to follow, were nonetheless clear and coherent. It is liberating to think for yourself. It's also hard—exhausting, even—to navigate your way through a complex world when nobody's telling you how to act or what to believe.

With the advance of secularism, many people in Northern Ireland are on a journey similar to mine: questioning, deconstructing, rejecting and reshaping the evangelical Protestant faith they've inherited from the generation before. The established Protestant Church is no longer the unassailable behemoth it used to be. While new, community-focused and predominantly charismatic churches emerge all over the North, the bigger and more established denominations increasingly look to be on the back foot. More and more people are ticking the 'no religion' box on our ubiquitous evaluation forms. The Political and Cultural Prods (those whose Protestantism is not tied up in notions of faith) continue to beat the same tired drum, militantly maintaining tradition is the best line of defence against perceived threats to their existence. (I quote here a sign currently displayed in East Belfast. Two masked gunmen flank the following statement: 'the prevention of the erosion of our identity is now our priority.')

The established evangelical churches seem to be thinking along similar lines. For the most part, they've adopted the atypical Northern Irish stance when faced with crisis or imminent change: a deep-seated refusal to budge from their traditional way of doing things. An inability to compromise. So, it's been no to marriage equality. No, to basic women's rights. A kind of muted, mumbling 'no, maybe, we'll think about it later' on issues pertinent to the climate crisis. I'm generalising here. There are progressive individuals within each denomination, doing their best to steer the ship away from the iceberg, but for the most part, the big Protestant denominations have stubbornly maintained outdated modes of thinking. As a result, they're haemorrhaging members. Most people in Northern Ireland are no longer satisfied with a worldview defined by the negative. The days of Paisley's blanket No to everything are thankfully behind us. Those of us who've retained some fledgling notion of faith, wish to contribute to church communities which are relevant, active and inclusive. Under these terms, most of the churches once considered immovable institutions are looking increasingly obsolete.

What does this look like in practical terms? Well, there's been a slow but steady withdrawal of Church presence in schools, with the 7 per cent of schools which are now integrated striving to maintain a neutral religious environment in our classrooms and assembly halls. Whilst the separation of church and state is far from complete— there are a number of Unionist politicians still citing personal religious belief as the primary influence on their politics—we no longer have ordained clergy holding office in government as was common during Paisley's reign. Neither is there the same degree of congregational support in regards to legislation which limits rights for women and members of the LGBTQ+ community. I have heard of congregations who were instructed, from the pulpit, how to vote in the Brexit referendum; and the degree to which para-church organisations like the Evangelical Alliance are still informing Ulster's believing Protestants how to think, lobby and vote on key political issues should not be underestimated. However, in comparison to the 70s, 80s or even 90s it is heartening to see a marked and growing separation between the evangelical Protestant Church and the politics of the North. A small number of extremely vocal, mostly fundamentalist voices remain, but the majority of people on the street seem inclined to keep religion out of their politics.

For people like me, whose experience of Protestant faith was not just religious but also social and cultural, the erosion of evangelical influence is extremely apparent in the waning visibility of traditions and institutions which thirty—or even twenty—years ago formed a kind of sub-culture for Born Again believers in the North. Amongst these I'd list uniformed church organisations for children, Sunday Schools, holiday clubs, mission trips and evangelical organisations like CSSM, CEF and Scripture Union which were once extremely active and visible in their attempts to share the Gospel with young people. There was also Manifest, a monthly youth gathering for young believers in the Ulster Hall, the massive weekly Christian Union meetings at Queen's University, and annual highlights like Summer Madness, Autumn Soul and New Horizons, Christian conferences and festivals which still exist though in a reduced, less visible form. The evangelical Protestant world of my youth conspired to keep young people busy and engaged in safe, spiritual pursuits where we'd be sheltered from the corrupting influence of the world. There were more than enough evangelicals in Northern Ireland—and in some communities like Ballymena there still are—to maintain a social subculture entirely distinct from the secular one. As the number of Bible-believing Protestants declines, it is becoming more and more difficult for these evangelicals to retain their institutions and separatist practices.

Part of me is relieved to see this finally happening in the North. The erosion of a pervading evangelical culture has led to some degree of progress in terms of gender and sexual equality, ecumenical endeavours, peacebuilding across the sectarian divide and further integration within our schools. It has allowed church-owned buildings which weren't being fully utilised to be re-purposed as useful community initiatives such as Belfast's Duncairn Arts Centre and the Skainos Centre on the Newtownards Road. It's also made it a little easier to challenge hypocrisy and bad practice within Protestant evangelical circles. As the established churches lose their overbearing influence, more and more people have had the confidence to address spiritual abuse, corruption and negative church experiences. Arguably this shift in the way we understand church has allowed hundreds of people, like myself, to nurture a faith which is not inherited or dictated. I am incredibly thankful for this and yet there's a part of me—a deeply buried Presbyterian part—which mourns the decline of the Protestant Church. Perhaps this sadness is not based upon reality so much as an idealistic notion of what church could have been: the tremendous potential which has been squandered in this place.

I'm thinking of all those brave, inspiring evangelicals who—often disregarding the denominational stance—strived to forge relationships with their Catholic neighbours during the darkest days of the Troubles. I'm thinking of those whose faith called them to be radical peacemakers fighting hard for ecumenical worship spaces, contending for integrated schools, and new inclusive institutions like the Corrymeela Community. I'm thinking also of the legacy of care, provision and practical service which the churches have established across Northern Ireland. Food banks. Mums and toddlers' groups. Senior citizens' luncheon clubs. An enormous network of organisations and activities for children and young people which often kept teenagers safe, engaged and less inclined towards other more negative ways of spending their time. I'm not suggesting the Protestant churches were the only, or even best, providers of these services—but a decline in both the finances and human resources coming from the church sector is already apparent in most parts of Northern Ireland. In East Belfast, where I live, many of the young people who roam the streets at night, frustrated because they've got nowhere to go would—two or three decades ago—have been attending church-run youth clubs, children's meetings or Boys' Brigade. The church in decline leaves a noticeable gap.

My father passed away a few months ago. During one of our final evenings together, we spent some pleasant hours paging through Judith Cole's photobook of Northern Irish mission halls. Dad reminisced about his childhood, pointing out people he'd known. We joked that every mission hall seemed to have the same burgundy tea set—wondering if they'd bought in bulk. My father grew up in Cromkill, a tiny townland on the edge of Ballymena. There were a handful of mission halls a stone's throw from his front door. He taught a Sunday School class in one. Many of the mission halls were still running when I was a child. Their names recited, sound like poetry to me now: Tullygarley, Slaght, Carnalbanagh and Leighinmohr.

In Cole's photos, they are humble constructions: wooden shacks with corrugated tin roofs, converted barns in farmers' yards, squat brick buildings in the arse end of nowhere, sheep and cows looking on. They are equally austere inside. Hard wooden chairs. A lectern for the preacher to speak from. Home-made curtains. A plug-in boiler for the tea. The ever-present sign insisting only the King James Version of the Bible should be used. These mission halls had their heyday in the years between the wars. They sprang up in rural townlands, usually financed by local folk. Mission halls allowed those believers who couldn't make it to a larger church to walk or cycle to a house of worship and fellowship there with their neighbours.

When I think of what's been lost with the decline of evangelical Protestantism it's the idea of mission halls which saddens me most. Despite all my issues with the Protestant faith I can still recognise that there's something true and dreadfully beautiful about worshipping alongside the people who make up your immediate community. The people whose land runs into yours. Who help with your harvest, expecting you to return the favour. Who are your first and last defence in times of trial, mourning and celebration. Whose children play and school with yours and might, one day, marry them. Each time you meet to sing and pray you must find a sense of fellowship with these people. Though you don't always see eye to eye, you're bound together by faith and geography. There's a deep and nuanced understanding of community at the centre of the mission hall model. This is the idea of church practiced well. It has the potential to find unity in the midst of difference. It offers security. And genuine care. I still believe an idea like this is worth holding on to. I believe it's worth contending for.

he brought it with him
Kerri ní Dochartaigh

His granny said: '*he brought his name with him, that one*', the first time she met our baby.

We were all huddled into the one-roomed stone cottage her son and I currently share with our son, right in the very heart of Ireland, just where the central bog has had to give way for what some might suppose to call 'civilisation'. A muddy laneway that crosses a ghost-line; the once-track that connected the north of Ireland to the south, once. A railway cottage that never has any phone signal, a million miles away from anywhere or anyone we know. Our wee dwelling is so small that there isn't even room for a sofa. The dog that came to live with us the morning after the foggy winter's night we moved in sleeps in a purpose-built nook my partner created for her in underneath our bookshelves. The bookshelves are slate grey, unintentionally mirroring the stone and the sky—and were also purpose-built. They are the thing that take up the most space in the whole house.

We have lived together, my lover and I, in three different houses before this one; all in the north of the island, in my hometown—the city of Derry. The internet tells me the average person will live in seven different houses in their lifetime. Before that winter our lives & bodies & days & belongings became intertwined as ivy on the old sycamore at the foot of our garden; he had lived in 23 houses and I in 34. We moved into this cottage two days after the Winter Solstice of 2019, a handful of weeks before the UK left the EU; another handful of weeks before the most life-altering collective experience many of us have ever known: the entrance of Covid 19 into our bodies & our nightmares; our consciousness & our world.

My partner inherited the cottage two summers before we moved in; right at the point we began to witness the slow, heart-wrenching unravelling of much that we had held dear in Derry. Brexit went at its achey, anonymous work in the North of Ireland long before its shift officially began, you see. It felt so obvious to us that we would simply move there: that we would change almost everything in our lives beyond all recognition. We did not really plan for it at all, so to speak. We fell into this new life without any real sense of having even talked any of it through; of having given such vast upheaval even a second thought. It was only us two, you see—back then; no matter how much or for how long I had longed for it to be otherwise—so we had only ourselves to think of. We walked away from all that we knew in the course of a single month, really. Packed up a rented home; shut down a small business; said farewell to the small group of people we felt close to. Somehow it felt like the most ordinary thing—and the wildest—all in one foul swoop.

We arrived at this new house in weather the like of which I had never really experienced before that night. I could not give one solitary jot about what might be referred to as *bad weather*: rain, hail, wind, snow, etc etc etc. I am very comfortable with the elements. I grew up on the northwest coast of Ireland so I was left with very little choice. I am a child born of the winter, and I remain drawn to that final season of our year, still. I am taken by storms, and I always have been. I am particularly drawn to winter storms. I am drawn to their light, you see.

I remember sitting through an English GCSE lesson in a cold Portakabin; hearing the opening line of *Jane Eyre* and imagining that it would stay with me always. Knowing that there is so much to be said of a moment in time that begins with wild weather; weather that will not be tamed; weather that stops you in your place and holds on to you for dear life.

And so it was with that storm that carried us across the border—north to south—to settle here in the very centre. Metallic clouds; lilac strips across a violent grey sky; a violet halo around the storm's winter moon. Even the birds knew the weather in question 'meant something'; so much more than what it really *should* have meant, of course. The starlings were the most clued in. They wheeled in the sky; trailing us as we tried to outrun them; all of us tucking our secrets in—beneath oxters that got wetter by the minute.

That very first night I began to dream of a golden bird being thrown around by a fierce-faced wind; hung with silver thread; from an unnervingly bright-white moon. The dream was unlike any I had ever really had before. The light in the dream was not really light, at all, in fact. It was more like a murmuration. The light was a gathering of iridescent birds; sharing something with me that I couldn't quite translate; beneath a brilliantly radiant, salmon-pink sky.

That first night I began to dream of a different kind of light.

A kind of light I knew, early on, I would never be able to walk away from.

I began to dream of a light that belonged to someone I had not yet met.

Light they would bring with them, from the very first moments when they arrived.

I am haunted by the light of things
that I have not yet even known.

There is no metaphor
at play here.

I have forgotten the layout of almost every home I have lived in.

Where the kitchen was. If the doors opened in or out.

If there was carpet or wood beneath my feet.

If the garden had a wall, or a fence, or a gate:
even if there even was a garden at all.

But I could describe for you in minute detail the
following things…

The way the light fell in every room of every home
I have ever lived in—in every season—at every time of
day. The light in almost every film I have ever watched,
and in every illustrated book I have ever read.

How it danced & sang & called to me.

The light I grew up with and then ran from over &
over & over.

Light from days of loss; from days of love; from days
of both. The light when the swallows arrived & then the
light when they had to leave in all the years that I've
noticed them.

The light in the Bogside on the winter's evening I fell
in love with my partner.

Light that threw itself down in sleety slants on his
overcoat as he walked away.

The way it made an old black & white movie of the
dreich Derry November night.

The light on the first morning many years later when
we woke up in our white transit van outside our current
home.

How it was like all the light in all the world must have
made its way here to this very laneway.

How it was like nothing I could really have believed

was true before.

How it took me the whole day to realise it was the Autumn Equinox, and how that shocked me to my core; in a way similar to waking up in a stranger's bed.

How home can be the back of a van on a fresh September morning, parked up in the back-end of nowhere—damp to your bones and desperate for coffee—as long as it is with the person you like to see in an overcoat best of all. As long as the overcoat wearer notices the light and carries you to its source, no matter the time, no matter the weather; in the back of an old battered transit van.

Light has been my only constant.

Light has been my guiding star.

Snow light.

Storm light.

Northern light.

Southern light.

Home light

Hope light.

I cannot get away from it, you see.

I cannot get away from light.

What our son's granny meant was that by coming with the full pink moon of April—the first moon of the second pandemic spring—he sang his name out for us like a song. She didn't say that, of course, those are not the kind of words she would really choose but I know it's what she meant—one way or the other. My partner's mother meant that when we named him for the Irish god of poetry & love & a golden river: it wasn't really *us* that chose it at all. She means that when we placed the Irish word for red straight after that one—just before his father's surname—we weren't really giving him anything that wasn't already his to claim.

You see *he brought them with him*, his names. They had always been his, perhaps since even before he arrived. From the very first moment we knew there was a creature inside me—the size of a poppy seed; brand new and somewhat surreal—something about the way that light worked changed. It has yet to go back to how it was before, and I am not holding my breath.

I peed on a white stick that night, as velvety darkness fell on a white day; one full of Connemara pebbles & sandpiper bellies & a folkloric crescent moon. There was no whiteness in the answer to our question though; the response to our call was blue as a cornflower, or indigo as it starts to fade, or the sea from far away. It was the blue that folk write books about; sing songs about; go crazy for. It was a kind of blue that made us switch on the outside light to call in the moths. The kind of blue that held us outside a while in the amber light that had just gone on outside our small stone home. A kind of light that gave us a chance to remember how to breathe.

Even when he was limbless & so tiny he would have slipped through the eye of the smallest needle, he had already brought something with him. Even before he became a real thing, something we could whisper of as autumn winds threw plastic pots around outside our window; long before we had to tell those we loved about the creature in my womb over zoom, even way back then he carried light with him.

He couldn't help it. It's who he is.

Even when we assumed he would not last, *it* would not last, the hope that had taken to clawing at our throats would not last; *even then* the light had changed forever anyhow. There was no going back to the lives we had lived before he came along. He grabbed us by our feet and hurled us into the garden. He shook us awake and he tickled our feet.

He reminded us to look at the moon, to look at the moon: LOOK AT THE MOON.

When we first moved to this laneway I foolishly imagined I would stay here forever. I even said so in a book; tying this false idea down onto paper; sending it out into the wide and unforgiving world. Being here made things inside me feel different. I no longer felt like I needed always to be running away.

What I didn't understand, back then, was that the only thing I was running from was me.

What I didn't understand, back them, was that the only thing I was searching for was me, too.

★

I knew he would come with the full moon. It was a pink one. An April one: the first full moon of the Spring. It breathed us all right in, as close to it as it could get us, and then spat us back out like the entrails of a bolshy sea.

Hare Moon /
Red Grass Moon /
Sprouting Moon /
River coming back Moon /
Fish Moon /
Moss Moon /
Egg Moon /Egg Moon / Pink Egg Moon
He brought his name with him, that one,
although it took weeks for him to share it with us.

This laneway is the only place in the world I have ever sown seeds into the soil, watched them bloom & unfurl, & then collected the seeds for the new year as the life inside them turned outside in. Never before have I known a garden this intimately as to know it in the winter; stripped & skeletal; so seductively & suddenly bare. It almost breaks me into wee small pieces; shards of glass; to think about leaving here; even though I know that we would be in a much better position as a family elsewhere right now. It's not about the house, or the laneway, or the county, or the island. I feel broken, I realise, by the thought of leaving the place we found out about the seed that grew into our son. The small stretch of land on which we stood with white plastic in our hands, a white moon in the sky, and a blue line singing out to us like fox cubs; like a promise; like the banshee. The place I sowed seeds into the earth the day before he came. The place I stood with him in my arms, me howling with confusion & with love; with fear & with hope; as meteors flashed across the postpartum belly of the sky. The place where I finally let go of all the guilt & the shame & the anxiety: this garden where I felt parts of me soften; pink & quiet. The place where I realised nothing would ever be the same again and that that was both harrowing and gorgeous all in one.

This garden where I became the only thing that I will always be.

★

I've long been drawn to Wabi-Sabi—a world view based on the acceptance of transience and imperfection that speaks to the Buddhist ideal of existence: nothing lasts; nothing is finished; nothing is perfect. Time and time again, since my son was born, I have felt that if anything could summarise the life-altering changes in me since becoming a mother—perhaps it is that idea. No given moment will stay forever, no worry or ache will remain always, every day offers fresh hope that things will be brighter; lighter.

You see *he brought them with him*, his names, our son did.

He was named for the moon & for poetry & for a wild river.

Impermanent things; unfinished things; imperfect things.

He was named for the red that followed him around like a song; that shapeshifted as each morning of his first week arrived; red that faded into pink right before my eyes.

Hues that I couldn't quite get out of my head: colour-worm.

He was named for a moon that never stood still long enough for me to photograph it after I breathed him out of my insides like a song.

Since he came along I have spent every journey we have made in the back seat of the car we bought when we knew he really was coming along. I've spent so much time in that space, one I had never been in before he came, that I recently dreamed I lived there.

Going through the 'Notes' section on my phone to garner gems to set in this piece, I found the following odd bullet point: 'BIRD OF LIGHT in the back seat of the car'.

One of the most beautiful experiences of my life made we weep like a baby but I would have forgotten it forever in my foggy matrescence haze, perhaps, without this note. When the summer sun was making its way away, far from us, my partner dragged us out of bed to go to the sea. I needed it more than I can put into words, really, and on the way home my phone made a shimmery, exquisite dance on the roof of the car. My son laughed a laugh I had never heard before—over and over—looking at me as though I had given him the whole world into his wee hands. My wee bird, laughing at a bird of light; in the back seat of our car. I'm not sure what it was that made me weep when I recounted it in my diary that night: exhaustion; emotion; overwhelm; joy?

Going through pictures on my phone later I discover that the only one out of 8679 that has HOME as its auto location is one of me in the same back seat. Only my lap is in the shot; a set of random objects are the true stars of the picture: a nursing shawl given by a dear friend when we struggled to feed, the bag I carry my son's things in, his favourite pompom hat, his first bear from one of the most beautiful women I know and the reusable cup I bought with my best friend at the last Port Elliott Festival; one of the last things I did alone before the world changed forever. I want to say more about this image, these objects; the sheer poetry of it all; the magic—but I am so tired—I am so caught up in the living of it, I suppose. These objects will not be around me forever but something about what they might represent feels like it could last a lifetime.

When I started this piece I had, only just that week, begun to write a book about learning to be rooted.

Alongside websites about trees and the psychology of staying, I had browsers open on my laptop listing beautiful old tenement flats in Glasgow in an attempt to move there with my family. Only a handful of weeks have passed since then but already the location has changed; we are considering Cornwall now, just as we considered Bristol before we considered Glasgow. Who knows where it will be next week, or if we might just use the wee bit of money we've managed to put away to buy a van and take to the road. This, for me, is a huge learning curve. The sense that HOME is not a place but an outlook, a feeling, a way of living. The idea that rootedness does not mean necessarily mean being held in one particular place. Perhaps, in fact, for some people, it is quite the opposite actually.

I feel at home stood at the sick sycamore at the foot of the garden of this cottage we live in now.

I feel at home looking at hidden Cornish coves on Instagram that I've never seen in real life.

I feel at home when I pass the Hospital where our son came into the world despite having no other connection to the town at all.

I feel at home in myself, despite how hard new motherhood is.

If I'm really honest, the place I feel most at home is in the back seat of our car—my son holding my hand until he falls asleep—my partner singing along in funny voices to songs on the radio; no matter where we are headed.

★

Perhaps motherhood is just another word for home.

Perhaps home is just another word for *safe*; or *content;* or *whole*…

I feel at ease; I feel full up; I feel like me.

I feel safe; I feel content; I feel whole.

I feel at home; I am your home; *I am home.*

Gradually Suddenly
Maria McManus

I think about dying every day. Several times a day. There.
I have said it now. Written it down. Scarred a page with
the fact. I have confessed. I feel ashamed about it, but it
is true. I ruminate on this without a moment's notice.
It is my default setting. I must actively distract myself
with other things if I am to function at all. All roads, all
stray thoughts, lead there. I notice it, set it aside, carry
on doing what I am doing. And then it comes again. I
know this now. I know the pattern well, and that it shifts,
disintegrates, reassembles.

★

    The neighbours' children said our mother was dead.
They had seen the bread van, our father's car, the smashed
windscreen, heard the screech of tyres, the collision, the
ambulances, our mother dead, they said, and our brothers
and father had been taken away. They might die too,
they said. I am six years old.
    I am sitting at the bottom of the stairs in the hall.

There is a 'stage' there; a semi-circular polished wood platform, with two steps further down into the hall. My father has returned home, bringing my brothers and the bag of our mother's blood-soaked clothes, but not her. *Surgery, loss of an eye, possibly both eyes, Altnagelvin Hospital, weeks, months, be good, behave, do as you are told, do your homework, don't fight, eat your dinner, clean up after yourselves. We'll see.*

He says he isn't lying. He might be... I want to believe him can't help believing that the Sweeneys and the O'Hares and the Veseys might be telling the truth. The Vesey's mother died, so *I know* mothers die. And I know that no matter how much homework you do, nor however many dinners you eat without complaining, and that even if you go to bed when you are told, and wash your face and teeth, and change your knickers and don't fight and do all the other things that you are told, and when, mothers still die.

★

In my school photograph from the time, I am a very sombre little girl. My hair is tied up tightly and pulled back in a ponytail. There are kirby-grips and clasps— things that nipped and pulled. I am wearing a dress that was only for wearing on Sundays. These things are evidence that our mother was not at home.

Normally, I'd have been defiant enough to refuse to

wear the dress, I would have chosen my own clothes, and I never would have left my hair tied up nor if I could avoid it, let it be brushed. Were my mother at home, she may have been too busy to intervene, and I could have gone to school dressed as I wanted to, with messy hair. I might have smiled.

Things were not normal anymore. Everything became a transaction. Be good, or else… Behave. I was banking compliance. It was speculation in that respect, with the only leverage a six-year-old imagines they have, influencing things beyond their control: Be good = return of mother. Being 'good' was hard, tense, anxious work. I didn't dare drop my guard for a moment.

The neighbours' children were mistaken, and our father was not lying. When our mother eventually came back, she had cuts on her head, scars on her face. She wore sunglasses all the time, night and day. Peters and Lee were popular, as were Roy Orbison and Stevie Wonder; they wore sunglasses. Jacqueline Kennedy Onassis also had sunglasses, and a similar sad glamour. Sunglasses were 'in'.

When our mother slept, one eye, the glass one, always stayed open.

I'm watching yiz, brats.

Tiny fragments of glass worked their way out of her skin. As she watched television, she absent-mindedly worried the skin on her forehead and cheeks and chin with her fingertips, working minute splinters to the surface. She'd jump if any of us approached her on her left side, our presence appeared sudden to her, terrifying her and so unexpected you might get a 'scud on the lug' for doing so.

'Youse skitthers, you scared the bloody life out of me!'

She had eight kids under the age of eleven, a dog she didn't want, a swaggering husband with notions. It was hard being married to a bigshot. My parents eroded each other's lives constantly. When their disappointment and rage was in full spate the walls of the house my father built contained them, but only just. It still spilled out, each child a tributary.

I spent a lot of time in the dark, under the stairs, in the hot-press, in the bottom of wardrobes, under my bed, behind the settee, anywhere the sounds of the world could be attenuated and muffled. I could close my eyes, but I couldn't close my ears. When I closed my eyes to go to sleep, ghouls appeared, shapeshifting out of the murk in reds and greens and cobalt.

I made up soundless stories in gesture. Shadow puppets in the beam from a lamp. In one of my early reading books there were instructions and pictures of how to make a rabbit shape, a wolf, a swan, a butterfly— the alchemy of light, my hands, the dark, here the story of Red Riding Hood. How dark it was in the belly of the wolf. Here, Jonah, because it was dark in the belly of the whale. A bible story of golden honey and bees in the dark bleak belly of a dead lion. *It was also dark in the forest Hansel, wasn't it? Gretel? Wasn't it dark there? Talia, Little*

Briar Rose, when you slept for a hundred years, it was also dark there, wasn't it? Magic happened, the elves changed the fortunes of the shoemaker and his wife, but always under the cover of darkness.

Simple games with torches; behind the curtains, playing 'stage', or 'make-it-up' with a model theatre, a proscenium arch of card and balsa wood, lush images of curtains, and paper characters on wee pokey sticks. It was all play.

Later, as a teenager, I was wandering country roads at night. I grew up on the northern side of the Irish border. It was to be expected that there was, let's call it, 'drama' going on out there in the dark. I was an 'extra' on that set; the 'war' was men's business.

I went about my business, terrified but doing it anyway. Getting from A to B was what I needed to do, and walking was the way to do it. And the men, if they were out there, had to assume themselves under surveillance from their own enemies, and they needed all their attention for saving themselves. Mostly they were leaving me, a bit-part player, alone.

Of course, I was afraid, always, but I had strategies—looking for pinpricks of light from houses scattered across the landscape, counting the steps between home and the crossroads, then starting over, counting between one house and the next: the crossroads to Mrs Farmer's, her lane to Docherty's, Docherty's to the Leonard's. House lights were always some indications that friendly others were there, existing, reachable, signalling their presence in the night. When I was lucky there were stars or the moon.

I was hidden, concealed, and felt safer somehow in the dark. If I was detected by the night-sights and infrared cameras of the army, I was at least of no interest to them. I was stealthy, listening, often walking blind, sensing the route with my feet: the verge, the lane, grass, tarmac, concrete, gravel. Hidden. Hiding. Safer, somehow, despite the scruffles in the hedgerows and the coppices of trees—these were 'always'/'probably' badgers, foxes, herds of cattle or sheep, not men on the run, nor security forces on manoeuvres out to get them.

I have only experienced absolute darkness once. I was down the Marble Arch Caves on a residential school-trip. It was odd to be on a school trip three or four miles from my house, but I'd never have had the opportunity to go in there otherwise. Marble Arch was not a show cave then. Our guide encouraged us to switch off the lamps we were wearing on our heads so we could experience pitch blackness, the absolute absence of light. It takes a while for the last visual images to fade from the retina and to adjust and really see the dark.

He encouraged us to listen. It was a cool, cold place, damp, and full of the sounds of water on stone. There are three rivers running through it, Shruh Croppa, Aghinrawn, also known as the Monastir, and the Owenbrean, the drip-drip seeping through minute cracks in the limestone. The cave system could flood suddenly, with enormous volumes of water running off the bogs and Cuilcagh. Episodically the three rivers in spate converged thunderously underground, pounding the rocks, and flooding every void. Three hundred and forty million years of spate and ebb and flow and drops of water on and through the cracks in sedimentation. The rocks gave way gradually and sometimes catastrophically and suddenly, making new beauty in the absolute unknown dark— cathedral-sized spaces that echo. Slow accretions creating stalagmites, stalactites, cave pearls, galleries, cascades, striated, glittering and damp. Runnels of water constantly seeking and finding the locus of escape, freedom, ready always to overcome resistance, to change direction to find the way, obstructed but ultimately borderless, and keeping moving. The stubborn strength of stone, resisting and resisting, and yet conceding at molecular level, because it can't not. It has no choice, as water too has no choice, as darkness has no choice, as light has no choice, as the breath in my body has no choice, until change is forced or happens simply because it must, because it is time. Simply.

Hyper-vigilance is to the traumatised as water is to rocks in a cave system. Erratic, destructive and omnipresent.

Trouble when it came, rumbled, cascaded, escalated, overwhelmed everything in its way—

the slammed door, angry voices, screeching tyres, smashing glass, a prodromal static silence that presaged my father's unpredictable but familiar rages, a car going off the bend in the road at our house, marching feet, Orange bands, the sounds of rioting, the suck/silence/boom of a bomb blast over the lake, shots, helicopters, sirens.

Extreme fear is quiet and compliant. Like when I was in an ice-cream shop with my young daughters and a bomb went off a few hundred yards further down on the Lisburn Road. *'Come on kids and we will just go home.'* My friend, a woman from Dublin, thought my lack of urgency and panic, odd, callous even.

People could have died in that bomb, she said with incredulity.

I know. Come on kids, let's just go home.

I learned early, to put a skin on fear. Feeling it could come later, when the children were safely home again, when the door was closed. When there was time, and space.

When I am in flight/fight or freeze mode I taste metal in my mouth, and have a sensation like needles on my tongue, across the roof of my mouth and in my throat. I expect to have to disappear and quickly. The bigger the threat, the cooler the head, the higher the threshold of compliance. *'Come on kids, let's just go home.'* Fear, like rage and power, can be subverted underground.

Pregnant with my first child, night after night I stole downstairs to the bathroom in the dark. *Keep the lights off because the men who robbed the bank while I was in it, know where I live, know I went to the police, know I have touted, and given evidence and they are bound to be watching this house.* But if I just keep quiet and slip about this joint with the lights off, I am safe. Under-slept, angry, impotent with rage and fear, but safe.

When paramilitaries tried to assassinate our neighbour in the night, I carried my baby around my house in the dark—if she was in my arms, she was most likely to be quiet and content and I could try to keep her safe. She and I could hide.

Besides, in my mind a moving target is harder to hit, and when the sinister phone calls came, well I could still crawl across the floor casting no shadows at the window, or I could ghost along the walls. Keeping the lights off inside is all the better to see out, shadow-seeking, the flare of a match lighting a cigarette, the sheen of moonlight on a rifle. Figures. Cowards. Wreckers.

I learned to recognise anxiety in myself, from a cowering dog. I found Basil at a beauty spot—a place people went to watch for seals. By then I had primary-school children, and we lived at Strangford Lough. He'd been abandoned there. I remember reaching for him, seeing him frightened and suspicious of me and I was aware that if ever he was going to bite me, it would be at that moment, not through viciousness, but because he was afraid. We let the warden take him anyway; there was no plan for a dog in our family—it wasn't practical.

There was a week of pester-power, hyper-ventilating

and howling from my daughters about how I had 'put-that-dog-on-death-row'. I caved, went to the pound, and bailed the same dog I'd rescued and had for free.

The vet who assessed him was right. We would have been better off with a pup instead, and everyone could have grown up together. Had we gotten a pup, there is a fair chance we would have had a dog that could have been house-trained, and didn't have separation anxiety and a skin condition, and one that wasn't hyper-vigilant and that didn't bark all day… and all night. And we could have chosen a dog that would learn to come when it was called. We could have had a dog that walked contentedly on the lead, one that understood that dog beds were for dogs and settees were for people, and one that understood it would be fed regularly and not have to scavenge relentlessly—no bin, nor salad bowl, no loaf of bread, no dish of butter, no gift of cheese, no piece of cake, no bar of chocolate, nor bag of cherry tomatoes, nor sausage could be left unguarded after Basil took up residence. The *Ginger Whinger* barked, crapped on the sofa, pissed on the carpets, jumped out the upstairs window, stole chips and ice-cream out of the hands of toddlers in prams, and followed me everywhere. Yes, even to the loo. He was rogue and unbiddable.

'*Give in,*' the vet said, '*You may let him up the stairs to sleep in your room.*

He's hard-wired and traumatised. He can't change. End of. Comfort him.'

He was the family dog for many years. We even got him a spaniel companion, but right until the end of his life, he flinched when we reached to stroke him.

★

I inherited seventy-three pounds fifty, from my father. He wasn't much older than I am now when he died. I spent all of it on daffodil bulbs. I planted them the same day I bought them, working through the dusk into the night, digging them into the cold, sodden sullen earth. I wept, crawling on my knees, wet and cold, determined it would be done, once, and all on the same day.

When the flowers came, they were defiant and feisty. Triumphant and rowdy. Joyous.

A small house is built there now. The daffodils are gone. I left and I don't go back.

In Hemingway's *The Sun Always Rises*, Mark Campbell explains that when he went bankrupt, it was in two ways, gradually, then suddenly. Change is like that; gradual then sudden. The end of my childhood was like that, as was the end of my first marriage, my mother's accident, and my father's death. So were the births of my daughters. So were the ceasefires, and the Good Friday Agreement, and Brexit, and the making of the caves, and the making of peace. Gradually and suddenly.

I flinch easily, startle readily. I don't like surprises and need constancy, calm, quiet, predictability—no sudden moves and rest cures lying in a darkened room. Nothing lasts. It is good that this includes sadness, unhappiness, and anxiety. Comfort yourself.

I have a plan. For when I die. I am on the donor register. I was squeamish about my eyes, but I know someone who has the gift of sight because he has donor corneas. So, now, eyes and all, all spare parts as may be useful to someone. Reuse/recycle.

The rest of me is to be buried in as compostable and as non-contaminatory a way as is possible. I want a tree; a crab-apple or a rowan, or both. The pretty crab-apple, with its beautiful flowers in the spring, blossoms that will bring the pollinators. Its fresh new leaves, the apples, the beautiful red apples that come in autumn and linger and fall—small, red bitter little apples, that the thrushes and the blackbirds love. Surely, they will come. May I have crocuses? And snowdrops? Daisies and dandelions? I am done with daffodils, but I would like anything that self-seeds and flourishes and feeds the pollinators. I want them to visit and return. May I have bluebells and hellebores if the spot is shady? A honeysuckle through a nearby hedge of briars or hawthorn? Can I have this place? If I am in earshot of the sea, this will be beautiful. And if an urban place, somewhere the swifts return. No stone is necessary. I will accept a stone if my loved ones prefer it but let's make it a birdbath, functional and un-shouty; it will be beautiful. Tanalised copper could also look good instead. Something curved and lippy, collecting rainwater, overflowing from time to time, capturing a sky ruptured by fledglings, thirsty scavengers, dusty little sparrows. Such things.

When I was a teenager, we used a huge, galvanised corn bin as a water trough for horses. Water boatmen always took up residence, diving down to the bottom when the meniscus was disturbed and broken by a child's hand, the muzzle of a pony, a pebble, a seashell, a wildflower plucked from the side of the road and dropped to float there. The image of the sky shattered, disintegrating and rippling. I could create an earthquake in the insects' water world, causing a tsunami, just by walloping the side of the corn bin with a crop, a heavy stick, a smallish boulder. And I'd watch a while as the picture of the sky and clouds rearranged itself, and how the insects rose again, and small leaves fell, settling on the surface. I have learned eclipses reflect on glass and water, and that it's safe to look at them this way. So, I need a bird bath at my grave, for each eclipse that comes hereafter. The world will keep turning, there will still be stars in the sky, the snow will cast blue shadows, there will be the moon, comets, eclipses, auroras, meteor showers, shooting stars. A birdbath will serve the birds but also capture the night, the seasons, the weather, the change of light and dark.

They say that when you die, all the dogs you've ever owned come running to greet you.

Everything will be gradual. And sudden.

Impermanence Way
Nandi Jola

I come from a city in South Africa that has had four different names, each representing a century of sea change. Port Elizabeth, with its monuments, is a reflection of the British Empire of the eighteenth century. In the nineteenth, we renamed the city Ibhayi, using our Xhosa language to resist the attempts of our Dutch-Afrikaner oppressors to erase the past. Late in the twentieth century, a new era dawned for a rainbow nation, and my city became Nelson Mandela Bay; and now in the twenty-first century, we name the city Gqeberha. This is a Xhosa word used to refer to the Baakens River which flows through the city—and this new name is also reflective of a flow of people, coming from all over the continent to live in South Africa.

If I had known that Northern Ireland is a land of impermanent things, I would have started writing sooner. I thought coming here was a way of looking at change through a different lens. I know the Irish people understand too well the pain of migrating: I think of the wakes of the nineteenth century for people going to America, a ceremony of mourning for living people as if they were dead, with the village becoming a shadow of itself, the loss of an indigenous language due to colonisation. Yet I have learned here that we can't put time to healing or full stop on the past, nor can we forgive and forget. After all, all these things the 1998 Truth and Reconciliation Commission in South Africa tried to do; in Northern Ireland, meanwhile, such a Commission has been—to date—rejected.

I was 20 years old when I watched the Truth and Reconciliation Commission in session. I was livid, I was filled with rage, I cried inconsolably. I was 23 years when I moved to Northern Ireland, and I was still raw inside. I moved from a hot country to a cold one, from brown fields to green ones, from a place overcrowded into a state of being exposed, from many languages to just one, from knowing many people to not knowing even one. My senses responded to this impermanence I was experiencing. I fixed my time to this change: *five years*, I told myself, *no more and no less.* My logic was: I had a five-year work permit and that's what it took to obtain citizenship, a British passport; so I was going to have two passports—and with these, I would navigate the world.

As it turns out, 1998 was a big year in both of my parallel universes. It was the end and the beginning of my journeys, as I began a move from old to new, searching for answers that are well hidden in the memory of us, buried in the landscape—but ever-present in our consciousness.

Listen to this quotation from *A Human Being Died That Night*, Pumla Gobodo Madikizela's account of apartheid South Africa:

> When Eugene de Kock, commanding officer of the apartheid death squads, was sentenced to 212 years for crimes against humanity, the black South Africans outside Pretoria's Supreme Court cheered and danced: the killer who had been nicknamed 'Prime Evil' by his own men would stay behind bars until the day he died. But one woman, plagued by the awkward questions about the nature of vengeance and forgiveness, decided to look into the monster's heart and found a man worthy of a pardon and freedom.

I walked away from all that: in fact I flew over 8000 miles—only to be met by Nelson Mandela on the Falls Road in Belfast. I felt a sense of joy, a freedom and emancipation. I shouted *Viva! Amandla!*

I was 23 years old when I arrived in Northern Ireland; 23 years since the signing of the Good Friday Agreement—and now I wonder to myself and I ask this place I call home: what advice would I have given to my 23-year-old self that I can offer here to a broken people who are, perhaps, on the mend?

Well, I would speak of inclusion. Women and children

were left behind at the signing of the Good Friday Agreement: this, even though it was women who shaped communities when the Troubles were rife, who built bridges, who opened community centres and crèches for children to play together and built a sense of belonging. When men were in prisons, the women kept going amid hostile environments—and yet both women and children were left outside when it came to the big moment. This happened in South Africa too.

I would mention the murals. In 2020, a George Floyd mural was defaced in West Belfast—and shortly after came condemnation and a statement from Féile an Phobail declaring that 'Belfast will never back down to racism'. I replied to that: I said that a people that voted against dropping fines for Black Lives Matter protestors that were being investigated as terrorists under the Serious Crimes Act of 2007—well, I said, where is the solidarity in that? How can this be a place that claims to be not racist?

I would mention the peace walls. In 2013, Northern Ireland's government set up an initiative to remove all of them by 2023—and yet today, approximately 116 barriers remain. So 116 barriers will be removed in two years? I know this is not realistic, not amid an atmosphere of rising tension, with the Northern Ireland Protocol and the Irish Sea border in place. In Northern Ireland, we keep finding ways of closing people in, of trapping them. These walls: they become a symbol of protest, of resisting change and of control. Newcomers find themselves settling amid an air of stagnation.

And I would mention Brexit, and the importance today of belonging, amid our swirling atmosphere of hate speech and division. In the book *The Good Immigrant*, Nikesh Shukla highlights the racism unleashed by David Cameron's referendum, and asks: 'What's it like to live in a country that ... doesn't want you unless you win an Olympic gold medal or a national baking competition?' I would bring that question forward—to now, to the year we saw Marcus Rashford being racially abused for missing a penalty at Euro 2021. This was a moment when England might win a major football trophy for the first time since 1966, and here was a Black man carrying the hopes of a nation—the same nation that booed Rashford each time he took the knee. Does he belong? Do we belong?

*

In 2013, the UN General Assembly adopted Resolution 68/237, by which it proclaimed 2015-2024 to be the International Decade of People of African Descent, with the theme *People of African descent: recognition, justice and development*. What does that mean? Well, it means that the international community is recognising that people of African descent represent a distinct group whose human rights must be promoted and protected. In a Northern Ireland context, how does this work?

Here are some ways to effect change, to turn our seemingly permanent ways of regarding the world into impermanent ways, to unfreeze our thoughts and have them melt and flow instead.

Let's talk about public history.

Is Northern Ireland even ready to talk about decolonising the curriculum? This is a conversation already happening in England, Scotland and Wales. Decolonisation is defined as 'the withdrawal from its colonies of a colonial power: the acquisition of political or economic independence by such colonies': but in Northern Ireland, we saw the Centenary of Partition service in Armagh causing controversy, we saw banners in support of Soldier F erected in such places as Portadown—in other words, right in the places where decolonisation conversations must take place. It happens that I acted as a Mentor on *Twenty-One Artists of the Twenty-First Century*, a programme for young artists who help to shape Northern Ireland simply by writing about it. I myself attempted to write about it: my screen film 'Partition' made it to the Belfast Film Festival 2021; I am constantly asking questions on public history. In wider society, Belfast City Council approved a proposal to erect a statue to the noted abolitionist Frederick Douglass—and a Douglass history trail through Belfast is one move in Northern Ireland towards a discussion of decolonisation and public history.

And yet, *To Kill a Mocking Bird* is still on the school curriculum in 2021. Here's a suggestion: let's make the seemingly permanent, impermanent. Isn't it time we introduce Emma Dabiri's *What White People Can Do Next* onto the curriculum?

Oh, and Emma, by the way, is Irish.

So yes, let's talk about public history.

Let's talk also about health, and about Covid.

Migrants, you know, are more likely to live in poverty. More likely to breathe illegal air-pollution levels, to work longer hours in insecure, low-paid jobs. To have short life expectancy: migrants are only here to work and die. During the pandemic, migrants have been expected to overwork, whilst citizens have enjoyed benefits such as furlough—and this has been a grim reminder that the British Government is not willing to budge on the question of equal rights for all. Migrants who have visas limiting them from claiming recourse to public funds even during the pandemic, have no choice other than to go out there and work in the middle of a public health disaster—even if it kills them. And we soon saw the changes applied to the Immigration Law and Refugee Law, making it more cruel and inhumane than it has ever been. As people panicked to buy toilet roll and emptied shelves, there was no thought of the migrants working inhumane hours and conditions, who would at last find time to go to these same shops—only to find nothing on the shelves. Migrants depend on food banks, even though they have jobs. It makes me laugh when I hear UK citizens calling themselves 'Brexit Refugees'. This is white privilege.

So, let's think about our permanent rights, and about those who have none.

And let's think about our identities.

As a poet I find myself looking at Seamus Heaney's poem 'England's Difficulty', and reflecting that I share some of the sentiments that he explores. Where do I stand in Northern Ireland—as a migrant, a writer, a contributor to society? I know very well, as Heaney knew, about the borders created to control people: yes, I think of those impermanent so-called *homelands* of Ciskei and Transkei in South Africa. The continent of Africa of course had *no* borders until it was colonised, the 1884 Berlin Conference regarding Africa a place of opportunity for some—and slavery for others. And I am too familiar with smuggling items across the border—although my borders differ from those of Heaney, for to me they symbolise opportunity, citizenship and class. Take my own daughter who was born in Antrim in 2003: she was refused British citizenship at birth—but gained Irish citizenship by default of law. She too crossed a border.

I have to cross the Irish border each time I want to visit the South African Embassy in Dublin—and I wonder each time if I will be stopped and asked to show my papers: for we know, don't we, that the border crossing is a risk to migrants and to people without a regulated status. Travellers—migrants—cross the border, and are taken from the buses and detained. It is cruel, especially when we can see that economic need forces people to cross borders in search for more opportunities. Partition and the border, in other words, means something quite different to such people; and partition and the border impacts on lives in ways that bruise and sting. And so the Protocol, and the Irish Sea border: these officials police not only the movements of goods, but also the rights of people born outside of Northern Ireland who have multiple cultures, identities and cultural beliefs.

I watched the Ireland's Future conference which took place in November 2021 in Dublin's Mansion House, and I listened to the words of prominent Muslim leader Shayk Umar Al-Qadri as he looked into the days to come— and I saw *The Irish Times* headline the following morning reporting his comments: 'Minority communities in North would vote for united Ireland'. And I remembered Heaney, and the last line in his poem: 'I crossed the lines with carefully enunciated passwords, manned every speech with checkpoints and reported back to nobody'.

And when I think about identity, I see more and more clearly that Northern Ireland needs hate crime legislation, and needs to be serious about the implementation of the Racial Equality Strategy. If we are going to move into a space that belongs to everyone, then the best time to start is *now*. Tokenism is not the answer. The news headlines proclaim that Northern Ireland is the racism capital of Europe—and yet we keep thinking that racism is an American problem, we keep thinking diversity is about cultural festivals and that's it—and we keep asking *When are you going home? …* as if this is not home.

Where are you really from?—people say. This is discriminatory—and yet, no matter how many times this is said, we are always expected to *wind our necks in*, to *blend in*. They say, *Oh, we don't see colour*—and the danger is everywhere in these micro-aggressions. Why do we call children born here *newcomer children*?

And let's think about our climate future.

Once again, you know, Africa is set to be the saviour of the western world. The electric car revolution that will save our planet and us will be driven by coltan, mined in Africa. This tale lacks one truth, yes, we are still omitting the facts: for while coltan is mined in Africa and exported to the West, in the same moment Africa is becoming a dumping ground for Europe's problem with diesel cars. The scrappage schemes aimed at convincing people to move towards greener solutions is not eliminating the problem, but only shifting it, and dumping in onto the people who did not create it in the first place. Simultaneously, our attitudes and language refer to these same Africans as *poor* and their homes as *third world*. I as an African cannot think of a bigger lie. I remember charcoal and mud being the foundation of my youth, I remember walking and planting and tending a vegetable patch, and I didn't wait on the West to tell me how to save water, because I had my water tank and the rain did the rest. Africa saved the planet that everyone ruined: and now whilst we pretend to save the planet by dumping our toxic waste onto Africa, we must soon realise that we co-exist.

We must dissolve these, our permanent identities and mindsets. We must mould new ones.

Are we doing this already? Well, if you asked me how many ethnic minorities are living in Northern Ireland, I would say *many*: since settling (and unsettling) here from 2001, I have seen churches, hairdressers and grocery shops and restaurants pop up in the Botanic area of Belfast. But the real question is: where is the *interculturalness* in that? Because I also see a Northern Ireland that is actually dividing further into ethnic groups of peoples. I see communities living parallel lives—and this is not a good thing, and it makes Northern Ireland an even more difficult place to understand. How will we learn, how will we predict the future in a society in such flux? The key is, perhaps, that *nothing* is permanent here, everything keeps moving, there is no way of ever establishing a definition of what this place is or imagining what it will become in the future. This sense of impermanence has been the hallmark of this part of the world for over eight hundred years!—and not simply part of the identity of the new Northern Ireland for a mere one hundred years. History and legacy are endlessly contested—as we saw when the President of Ireland declined to attend the church service at Armagh—and there are two of everything at the top: two passports, two heads of states, and two languages. So maybe we should follow what South Africa did and recognise all the languages in the Constitution—or, maybe not.

I always joked about moving from the frying pan to the fire. At times nowadays, I feel the heat more than ever, even though I have never been caught in the crossfire of bullets. And of course I have definitely been asked: 'What brought you here?' At times I want to borrow the reply of the British MP David Lammy and say, 'I am here because you went there first'; while at other times I tell a love sob story that people find hilarious. Because we all need to laugh and find common ground at times, find moments of winding a neck in and taking the craic whichever way it comes.

As a writer, I reflect a lot on paper, understanding that we need stories of lived experiences to make it into the curriculum, that we need books on shelves and films and in all walks of life that will reflect an endless movement of time and people. Because Irish people are emigrants and immigrants too—and even the formation of the population in today's Northern Ireland was partly though the movement of people from England, Scotland and Wales.

In 2021, the Irish say that they never enslaved anyone—but I challenge you to look into the dark secret of Direct Provision and tell me that this is not a form of modern-day slavery. As Frederick Douglass puts it: 'The Irish, who, at home, readily sympathize with the oppressed everywhere, are instantly taught when they step upon our soil to hate and despise the Negro. Sir, the Irish-American will one day find out his mistake.' I wish that these words were not true and I wish that the Irish had not learnt to hate not only abroad, but at home as well. For today, people speak of *them ones* and *foreigners*, as if the rest of the world has not seen the emigrant Irish.

If I was of any influence to the people of Ireland I would say this: there is more that unites us than divides us.

I would say this: building a nation takes all of us.

In my poem 'Tapestry of Love', I say:

> Let us give love a chance, to give our children
> hope of a world without hatred, where black
> and white walk hand in hand, let the peace walls
> come down, so that the ghost of apartheid can be
> finally laid to rest, for history to remain history
> only to be found in books on shelves.

If *our* home is to be a place, if it is to be *our* place, then let us start by not blaming or pointing a finger at the other person. Instead, let us listen to the hurts we all carry in this melting pot of a place. For we are all the makeshifts, the bystanders, the blow-ins, the rejects, the refugees, the asylum seekers, the migrants.

We are us.

We are resilient, we are the heartbeat of this place, we can create our rainbow flag and compose a new national anthem for ourselves.

So, let us in.

There was never a right time to look at regret.

Peace is never too late. Let us not turn it away, unwanted.

Klondike
Neil Hegarty

Here at the mouth of the river, I see a vast dome of sky.
To the north, the sheer scarp of Binevenagh mountain,
its basalt cliff-face silver-tinged today, though in certain
lights I have seen it shine a bright lustrous gold. To the
south, the docks of Derry: pylons and winches, and a few
minutes ago, a vast Polish container ship gliding silently
along the navigation channel, just a few cables away; I felt
I could reach out and touch it. To the east, I see the high
walls that keep the sea from inundating the sloblands—
the polderlands—of County Derry, from the deep black
soil of which the Broighter hoard of gold was unearthed
a century ago and more; and to the west, the land ripples
and rises into the Inishowen uplands. In the distance I see
the blue peak of Slieve Snacht: snow mountain, which
will indeed soon enough be dusted with a little snow.

For this is October, on the lonely and wind-scoured
edge of Lough Foyle. When I was here in June, the
swallows were darting and fluttering, and the larks were
wittering shrilly, and rising, rising into the luminous air
before diving again into their nests in the grass—long

green grass, marbled with yellow drifts of bird's-foot trefoil. But today, the swallows are gone, and the grass is etiolated and bleaching now as the year fails. Just here, just where the ships sail silently by, the river Foyle flows out into the lough; and just there at my feet, the turf falls down into the sea marsh, all raised banks and shallow waters, where wading birds live summer and winter alike. October: and the wind is—fresh, let's say, and getting fresher by the day; and any minute now, though the summer swallows are gone, the winter visitors—the brent geese and the whooper swans—will be arriving from Greenland.

This is a temporary landscape, this grassy expanse on the southern shore of Lough Foyle. It is strictly impermanent. Like those polders over to the east, it has been embanked and protected from the sea; it too is reminiscent of a Dutch landscape, lifted and draped across the soil in this northern district of Ireland. And it has changed, this landscape, and changed again. Twenty years ago, it was that unglamorous entity, a municipal dump just north of Derry's suburbs: clouds of gulls looking for pickings, and yellow machinery heaving and moving. Not a place to come for an autumn walk. Then, the council closed the area, and dealt with the waste, and slowly turned the land into something else, something more expansive and generous—into a refuge for birds and insects, with grass left uncut, and trees planted here and there; and even that salt marsh conjured marvellously into being; and there are paths running through the grass, for walkers to get out and taste the salty air, and feel the wind (keen and getting keener) on their faces.

And to look at that blue dome of sky, which reaches over the land and sea and distant basalt cliffs, and capturing, holding, retaining.

It looks permanent, doesn't it?——but I know that in the years to come, this landscape, a nature reserve today, will in all probability be abandoned to the sea, the whole expanse turned over to salt marsh, maybe. It simply may no longer be possible to hold the water back. The sea will reclaim this space, it will flow again where it flowed in years past.

Elsewhere, such a fact has already been accepted, and planning has begun; elsewhere, in even more marginal places than this, sea walls have been breached deliberately, and the water has re-entered and made itself at home. There are many virtues in such a state of affairs: breach the sea walls before the sea breaches them for us, and create managed marsh instead, that will flood and dry with the seasons; and act as a sponge, absorbing the force of the rising storms when they come, and providing vital protection for districts further inland. The swallows that nest here in the summer will have to look elsewhere, in such an eventuality——but the geese and other wildfowl will be pleased. More marsh, more salt, more room for us, they will say.

As I walk, then, and feel the hard path and firm turf

underfoot, I am not to be fooled.

It feels—odd to be walking across such an engineered landscape. Of course the whole lough and its shorelines have long been intensely engineered, intensely known: the first Ordnance Survey of Ireland in 1827 commenced at the mouth of the lough; the RAF surveyed the lough and the wide surrounding fields before building air bases there during the Second World War; Germany's surrendered U-boats were gathered together in Lough Foyle at the end of the war.

In addition, I know that all landscapes are engineered nowadays: they are constructed, and 'wild places' are a mere notion. Those blue Inishowen uplands in the western distance would be blanketed in trees, were the wild permitted to return; instead, they are bald and covered by heather, because our idea of what constitutes the 'natural' has today been deeply conditioned. Heather and bracken may look and feel right, but they're not natural.

Just the same, the flatlands in this part of the world— these great stretches of level fields which border Lough Foyle and Lough Swilly on Ireland's northern coast— feel extra-engineered, extra-odd, extraordinary. The Victorians built the sea walls, drained the marshes, created abundantly fertile farmland, designed and slotted in the sluice gates that maintained the new balance, and built the railways that were the real point of all this industry and activity. These landscapes are much quieter today: the trains still run across the Derry sloblands towards Belfast; but the Donegal rail tracks were lifted long ago; and walkers and cyclists use the level gradings, and birds forage in the flat fields. And now we have this new flat country park where I walk today—and this is most certainly engineered; a few moments ago I passed an information board, telling me with pride that the gassy, smelly heat rising from the sealed municipal dump below isn't escaping into the atmosphere to add to global warming; no, it's channelled, and harvested, and connected to the British National Grid.

Yes, it's not very wild, is it.

I come to these flatlands, in the course of my visits to my home place in Derry, to look about me. And there is plenty to look at; nothing, after all, can be hidden here. The weather can't be hidden: it gives fair warning of its approach hereabouts, the rain flowing like a shimmering, billowing curtain across the sea. Other walkers—for there are other walkers, this is not a world of WG Sebald in which there are no other human voices, or shadows, or company to be had; no, there are other people here, and their gambolling dogs, and in these flat fields they can't be hidden, they can be spotted five hundred metres away. And the sun itself can't be hidden: it breaks through the clouds on the distant blue hillsides and then sweeps across the flatlands, illuminating them like a spotlight, and then passes again.

I come to this new, engineered place for a view of

the sky—and of the water. Lough Foyle is underrated, or so it seems to me: tourists are drawn elsewhere, to the Causeway coast, or the Donegal uplands, not to these wide, shallow, silver-grey waters. But the lough is worth a sight—and here in the country park, a sight that opens suddenly upon one, magnificently, giddyingly. A sight that always opens suddenly, in my experience.

Coming over the hills from the east, the lough lies slicked across the distant flat fields. The other day, I visited with my father a church he had designed over there in County Derry. It was one of his first commissions, back in 1969. This church stands on a rise overlooking the Derry sloblands and the water: Star of the Sea is its name. We looked at the view, and then we went inside the church, and I put my eye to a circle of vivid modernist stained glass, and tried to look through the reds and the yellows, to see the lough.

From the west, the view connects with my childhood, with journeys home to Derry, following an afternoon spent visiting my mother's relations in Inishowen. Climb the last hill, and over the last hump in the road—and we'd say, There it is! On long spring or summer evenings, there was the lough, perhaps blue and perhaps silver-grey and perhaps shining in the mellow evening light, and there were the flatlands of the further shore. On winter evenings, a constellation of lights, of which I remember best the geometric lights of Magilligan prison shining hard and brilliant to the north, below the Binevenagh cliffs, and catching, summoning the eye, and bringing on a chilly thrill of fear. But no matter: for there were Derry's streetlamps glowing in the southern sky, and my father was making dinner, and we'd be down on the coast road and home in fifteen minutes.

And another layer of interest and oddness: as I look and scan and take a survey of the fields, I of course can't see this region's most obvious, most pressing feature. For there's the Irish border, just there, just on the other side of the salt marsh, that line that's invisible but that governs the geopolitical weather nowadays. Those blue Inishowen hills, just over there, are in the Irish Republic; I turn on my heel and look at the Derry polderlands, and these are in the United Kingdom. I turn again: the new salt marsh just down there, it's in the United Kingdom too, but its natural continuation fifty metres away is in the Irish Republic. I laugh aloud at the absurdity of a border in this joined, connected place.

Like the ship in the shipping channel, I can almost reach out and touch this border. It curls around Derry's suburbs as a cat's tail curls around its paws—although no, wrong analogy, for there is nothing warm, nothing comforting, nothing connecting or intrinsic about the border. And in Derry, it is always present, if never visible; it is always just there.

Although, not for much longer, maybe, if the forces unleashed by Brexit continue to work through our lives.

Yes, not for much longer, I am more and more convinced.

The changes we have seen, in just a few short years.

A few short years ago, I thought that this island of Ireland would be divided by the border for years, for decades into the future. I could not imagine any change. But now I can. Now, the ground moves beneath my feet. Now, our present dispensation crumbles as we watch, unable to believe the speed of change.

Now, I see a startlingly changed future coming towards us at a rate of knots, much as the weather sweeps across Lough Foyle, sweeps bracingly into our faces.

★

They say in Derry these days that Lough Foyle has become the new Klondike. I know why; and I laugh, I appreciate the analogy. The reason for the name lies, not in any seams of gold threading the shallow lough waters, but in the partition of Ireland one hundred years ago, in the unlikely unfolding of this new international border across the Irish landscape, from Carlingford Lough to Lough Foyle. This border was senseless: it made no sense at all on the ground, running as it did carelessly and nonsensically through farms and villages and even, on occasion, through people's gardens. It ran a plough through lives. It cut off towns and villages from their commercial hinterlands, and from its creation flowed a century of division and sorrow.

When it reached Lough Foyle, the border at least

stopped being senseless—which is to say, it stopped entirely, it stopped in its tracks; by which I mean that its line was no longer subject to any form of international agreement. The British view was that the entirety of Lough Foyle, all that great, silver, shallow bowl of water, must belong to the United Kingdom. The shipping channel from the ocean down to Derry, on the British side, ran close to the western shore of the lough—close to Donegal, the Irish side. To protect this shipping channel, so Britain must control the waters of the lough right up to the high-water mark on the Donegal side.

So said the British.

The Irish, unsurprisingly, said no.

And there the matter rested: a fraught point of geopolitics, unsolved, unsolvable, on the north-western hem of Europe.

It was Europe—in the form of the European Union— that applied a salve or balm of sorts to this festering situation: for the British and Irish accession to what was the European Economic Community in 1973 removed the problem. After all, in a common market, who cared where the border lay? The problem could go away now— and go away it did, for some decades. In the meantime, Lough Foyle was the scene for some Troubles-related activity: most spectacularly in 1981, when the IRA hijacked the coal boat Nellie M, bound for Derry from Glasgow, and sank her in the lough, just off the Donegal shore. My family, I suppose like every family in the region, took a spin down the coast to see the stricken ship, foundered in the water; Nellie M became a bizarre tourist attraction, until she was eventually dragged up and away and the shipping channel reopened once more.

When the dreaded Brexit arrived, however, these border salves could no longer be applied. It was still the case that nobody knew where the border was supposed to be, and now—worse and worse—this border separated two discreet economic areas. Where ran the writ, who controlled what, what about regulations and codes and health and safety? All this mattered—very much— because the shallow waters of Lough Foyle are not just there for me to gaze upon and admire. No: the lough is a crucible of economic activity. It supports a thriving shellfish industry: its muddy waters are rich in oysters. Indeed, the lough is one of the last strongholds of the native European oyster, which is today a rare delicacy; only limited numbers of the species are today landed and exported.

Klondike, though: what's Klondike? This comes from another element in the Lough Foyle aquaculture sector. The shallows on the Donegal side of the lough—these contested waters, these debatable waters—are lined these days with platforms, trestles, they are called, on which are grown Pacific oysters: larger, thicker of shell and altogether less delicate, less thoroughly superior than its native counterpart; and this industry is thriving and profitable. The mature oysters are harvested and loaded onto trucks for transfer to Rosslare and on to France, where they fetch high prices in the markets—but the authorities dare not intervene to control the industry, which therefore operates busily in a regulatory free-for-all, a grey area. A bonanza of oysters, a gold rush.

A Klondike.

How can this be? How can a whole unlicensed industry just exist there, in broad daylight, on the water's edge? A whole export infrastructure, a whole commercial ecosystem, right there, operating without any regulation at all?

The wild west, not half a dozen miles from Derry city centre.

The Loughs Agency, which is charged with regulating the valuable Lough Foyle fishery, dare not regulate the trade in Pacific oysters. Its website says—rather tetchily, rather tightly, or so it seems to me—that 'we have no responsibility for licensing or developing aquaculture in Lough Foyle. In Lough Foyle, the farming of Pacific oysters is currently unregulated.' And the Irish police, there on their very own foreshore, are constrained: how to operate there in the shallows and shoals, between land and sea, a region that on the face of it belongs to no jurisdiction, that acknowledges no law?

So, nobody intervenes on behalf of the oysters. These bivalves—and the suggested metaphor here is not lost on me, as I think of borders and of two sections, of halves and of edges, as I stand on a stitched hem, on a crumbling line between land and sea and scratch my head—these bivalves can pass through any hands concerned enough to farm them, can be loaded onto any lorry that cares to carry them, can sail the seas to France, and make fortunes for the people back home on the Klondike.

Yes: this is a strange present tense, here on these flatlands, amid these temporary fields and walls and dikes, and this shallow, silt-rich water. It is strange for the people who live here, for visitors, maybe even, who knows, for the wintering swans, and honking geese, for the Pacific oysters on their trestles, and the Foyle oysters on their ropes.

And how strange, to be alive and here at this moment in time, in this wilfully impermanent place, where change and decay are everywhere. Where climate change is already at work and perfectly perceptible to anyone who cares to look. Here on the water's edge, I feel October's keen north wind in my face, and imagine—but with good reason, with just cause, for has this not happened in Europe before?—imagine the world-changing assault that might come at any moment: the wind veers around to the north and becomes savage, a low-pressure system out in the Atlantic lifts a great dome of water above the surface of the ocean and pushes it into Lough Foyle, to sweep these contested lands away, to carve out new marshes, to sweep away the great sea walls.

It has certainly happened before.

It seems to me that place—these grassy fields and

temporary shorelines—dramatize or magnify the essence of time passing: that each moment crumbles, another and another, into the past, that we live breathlessly amid a present tense that we can never grasp or fully understand.

It seems to me that land and politics in this temporary place are in strange and gripping synchronicity. I think Klondike, a pell-mell, no order, no control at all. I think bivalve, the beautifully constructed oyster, with its two harmonious halves, working beautifully together, a symphony in nature.

It seems to me that the facts on the ground in this temporary place are no facts at all.

It seems to me that these flatlands—airy, wide, exhilarating—and these seas beneath their great dome of sky, are suggestive of a new way of thinking. They embrace volatility, they speak to the grain and the facts of our lives, and of our politics in this shifting, volatile part of the world.

Keep scanning and scanning, then: scanning the skies, scanning the horizon, scanning the tremendous expanses of temporary lands, to see the future coming towards us across the fields, across the water.

Sixteen
Paul McVeigh

1.

I was sixteen years old, once. A long time ago. It's hard to recall it. Lately, time itself has taken a turn for me. Whereas I used to remember everything, even small details, instantly, so much no longer exists. I reach back in time but my fingers move through air. It's as if being alive takes more effort, now; my brain needs more power to carry out daily life so it has started eating the past. You can't hold on to who you were, time takes care of that; experience changes you and the decisions you make do too. You can't even hold on to the memory of who you used to be, it seems. We are in every way impermanent.

But is everything impermanent? Well, we'd have to live forever to find out. Those who have their own children, I'm told, feel a sense of impermanence, that they have a legacy. What about the world we live in and the societies? On the surface it seems all is forever changing, some things don't seem to change very much at all.

2.

At sixteen, in Belfast, in Ardoyne, where I was born and bred, I liked girls—in the proper way. I liked boys, too, improperly, and that fact made life difficult for me, mostly because it seemed to activate a hatred in those who sensed it of me. I had little control over their discovery. It was as though they could see right into me, see my darkest secret and they didn't like what they saw. It took decades for me to perfect camouflage. To pass when needed, avoiding their disgust, hatred and, sometimes, violence.

Turned out my sexuality was fluid. I was one way, I was the other. I was both. Now, mostly, I am neither.

3.

At sixteen, I left school. It was an all-boys affair. Final tests were at that age, to determine your future. There were two options: to sit O-Levels, or, to sit the lower-streamed CSEs—a Grade 1 in CSE being equivalent to a Grade C (a bare pass) at O-Level. My school, however, didn't offer the option of doing O-Levels: students of St Gabriel's were only presented with the option of doing CSEs. We had no sixth form department, where over-16s stayed at school do the next stage of exams, A-Levels, required to enter university.

Being from Ardoyne, we weren't expected to sit O-Levels. We weren't expected to stay in education past sixteen—no college or university for us. Who from our area, our class, our backgrounds, would want to stay in school even if it were offered? Who would have been smart enough? Whose family could have afforded the lack of money going into the home?

Being the challenging, inquisitive type I discovered I could take O-Levels. I would just have to summon the nerve to make a special, formal request to the school principal to be permitted to sit an O-Level exam. It wasn't only that I would have to face my teacher of the subject and the school principal, but also my unforgiving peers. You weren't to be 'having notions' or 'ideas above your station'. Self-policing by those in your class was more effective than the discrimination by those in positions of power.

Did I mention, at sixteen, I was also bolshy, with a massive chip on my shoulder?

I made that special request to the school principal to sit an O-Level, although, I only had the audacity to ask to take one, in English Literature.

I got an A.

'Is that good?' I remember my mum asking.

4.

At sixteen, I went to the new world of the city centre,

to further education college. The world of school was gone, forever. I also now had daily leave from Ardoyne. The two places in which I had been stuck 24/7 for my whole life so far. What liberation! Anonymity presented a chance to rebrand myself. Not to be the person they had labelled me. My transformation started. Like a lifelong striptease, to reveal the self I would have been without their weight on me. The thrill of anonymity, bursting with promise, would soon take me to London for 25 years. What most people around me then seemed to fear the most was what I craved.

But first, I went to a college, right bang in the city centre, behind Belfast City Hall, to do the O-levels I hadn't done at school. I needed to pass these exams so that I could advance and sit A-Levels which would then allow me to go to university. I was always a year behind those my age: sitting my O-Levels late, sitting my A-Levels late, receiving my degree late.

At college, the students were of mixed gender and mixed religion and this was as I had expected. I was excited for this new world. I had previously only mixed with those of a different religion, and of a different class, knowingly, a handful of times. I had also expected to meet many ambitious working-class secondary school kids, like me, trying to get an education but, in fact, I met few. I was shocked to find the college mostly full of middle-class kids who'd failed at their higher level grammar schools and privileged private schools.

I gravitated towards girls as friends; if I discriminated against the boys, I didn't discriminate on religious or class grounds. Some of my new friends made my mum anxious for me. I remember her struggling to have a talk with me—the struggle came from the fact that 'having a talk' was a rare happening in our relationship but also due to the fact that mum left school at 14 to work in a mill at the bottom of our street and articulating her thoughts was something she found difficult. I have inherited the same lack of confidence, in that respect: it remains, to this day.

My mum wanted to warn me about stepping out of my class, that I should be wary of these new people in my life—these richer, middle-class friends. She warned that I shouldn't let these new friends pay for me in any situation, I shouldn't include myself in their activities because money would become an issue, and I should think of the position I would put myself in and what these friends might think of me for not being able to afford it. My mum knew, though she didn't say where she'd learned it, that negotiating class can be a tricky business, even when with friends and only for an evening out.

Although, now, many would assume I am middle class, I don't feel it—nor, I would argue, would my finances or living situations throughout my adult life have presented as middle class. And if class is as much in the mind, I can say that I've never thought of myself as anything other than working class. I think like a working-class man. I accept, however, that my 'notions' have gotten me places that most working-class people face many barriers to arrive at.

Thinking about the theme of impermanence, something came up for me. For most of those in poverty, and those in the working class—let's say those who have less: is their situation more permanent than those of higher classes—those who have more?

5.

I grew up in the height of the Troubles in Northern Ireland. I lived in Ardoyne, a large Catholic ghetto which was surrounded by Protestant areas. To prevent violent clashes, to stop 'invasion', to stop drive-by shootings etc we were, more-or-less, walled in—these barricades were called peace walls. Ardoyne was basically an open-air prison. Armed police and British Army soldiers patrolled the streets. The kerb-stones were painted in rotation, green—white—orange, the colours of the Irish national tricolour flag. These flags were also tied to some lampposts, hung from some windows. Some gable walls were painted with murals commemorating battles with the English in the past, some were memorials to local men or often children, killed by the current British Army. Near the peace walls the ground was covered in patches of blackened stains and broken glass from bottles and petrol bombs thrown during riots. Burnt-out cars and buses, that had been highjacked passing or trying enter

Ardoyne, dotted the area. Temporary barricades made by rioters blocked roads to stop or slow down the police and army. Half-knocked-down derelict houses and factories, their exposed gas pipes lit, broken drains and water pipes sent gushing streams down the streets, I could go on...

On the rare occasions I travelled outside across the city—a school trip, say—I saw that some of the immediate surrounding areas were Protestant ghettos, similar to ours—the colours on the kerb-stones changed red—white—blue, the colours of the British Union Jack national flag. There were murals memorialising similar events—only the names changed. It was shockingly similar—it was an education. Poor is poor.

Travelling through the city into wealthier areas I saw one of the most striking things that shaped my thinking for the rest of life—rich people didn't have the Troubles. I remember my young self thinking—'is it not enough that rich people have more money, better cars, better homes, go on holidays—but they are spared the Troubles too?' No army or police patrols, no painted kerbs or flags, no barricades or walls or brunt-out cars etc... they lived like people in the exotic dream-world I saw on the TV. I wanted a life like theirs (I hadn't known it was possible in Belfast) but, simultaneously, I resented these people and, to my eyes, their easy lives.

At one time, Ardoyne was called 'the biggest slum in Europe'. Time has brought better housing, and I don't see the level of poverty and desperate living conditions in working-class areas in general. But things aren't as rosy as they appear on the surface.

6.

About 9 years ago, when I was trying to get my novel, *The Good Son*, published, I was met with some resistance from the book industry because it was set during the Troubles. It was felt that it was a story already told many times. The most vocal resistance I came across was from other writers from Northern Ireland. It's interesting that the debate on this has re-ignited recently where a Northern Irish writer put out a challenge to her peers to stop writing about the Troubles. The main thrust of the argument is that the Troubles is old news and that by continuing to write about that time gives the wrong impression of the new Northern Ireland.

When I returned to Belfast, from London, about 5 years ago, I initially moved into my parents' house in Ardoyne. It was June, I think. What I remember vividly about that summer in Ardoyne is that there was a bomb scare in my street, that three men were killed by paramilitaries and three teenagers took their own lives within days of each other. I was disturbed, to say the least, by these shocking and what seemed like daily events. I decided to look past the veneer of the all-new, shiny tourist-friendly Belfast. Turns out Northern Ireland has the highest rate of teenage suicide in Europe, the World Health Organisation has classified the addiction to prescription drugs here as an epidemic, some inner-city areas have more than 50 per cent of the population on sickness benefit, I could go on. What have all of these facts got in common? Those mostly affected are the poor and the working class.

Belfast may change, but for working-class people, what lies beneath? Is their situation really that different? Northern Ireland doesn't have the Troubles unless you're living in a working-class area. And for those writers who don't want to talk about the Troubles, or, more boldly, don't want other writers to talk about it either, perhaps their distance from the Troubles comes from their distance from the working class, their areas, their lives and their current problems. This is not history, it is present day—not only in the hold the paramilitaries still have over these areas but also in the echoes on the mental health of the region with more people having died at their own hands since the Troubles ended than by the bullets and bombs during the war that was the Troubles.

Trauma and the impact of having less passes through the generations, some would say, genetically.

Healing can take generations, scars can fade, but some are permanent.

7.

At sixteen I joined the drama club at my further education college—we hadn't had one at my school. I needed an outlet for all the adrenalin that sixteen years of pent-up me was releasing. Trying on new people, shaping my body and the sounds coming out of my mouth to present as someone other than me. Many me-s that I could use to survive the outside world. To face it, thrive in it, beat it and own it.

And then—well, I don't know how I heard of it. I don't know how I got to the audition. I don't even remember the audition—but I remember the faces of my parents when I told them that the project was residential. If permitted, I was going to stay at a Queen's University hall of residence for their students for four weeks. It was in my city, twenty minutes' drive from my house, but I'd never been up that well-known road where the rich of the city lived. Later, I learnt that my mum used to clean a doctor's house there before I was born.

The Ulster Youth Theatre was an incredible experience. One that changed my life forever. For a start, it was the first time I was actually popular. My peers, who came from all around Northern Ireland: they liked me, they found me cheeky, funny, quirky and rebellious. My room became the common room where everyone hung out, talked all night, got off with each other, and became best friends for life: I joke here but, in fact, one cast member stayed in my life for twenty years and another became my best friend for over thirty years. Despite those extraordinary bonds and the lengthy, tangled life history, neither is in my life today, sadly. Something once unimaginable.

Proof of my startling newfound status as 'most popular', I dated the most popular girl in the group. In a production of *Romeo and Juliet*, I dated the stunningly beautiful and breathtakingly talented Juliet herself! I was in love for the first time. I was terrible at it. So unaccustomed to dating I was a nightmare. Jealous, clingy and controlling—and needless to say, it didn't work out. Again, I mixed with different religions and persuasions, the arts have a way of doing that, but, again, I found few from working-class backgrounds. Like I was to discover later in life, with writing, you have to be able to afford to be in the arts, especially if you want that for your career.

I had never seen a professional stage production, and I was stunned at the amount of work that went into creating a piece of theatre. For the acting alone, we had a voice coach and a fight co-ordinator, we studied the Alexander Technique and yoga, we worked with a choreographer, and a composer and director, both over from London—which was quite a thing during the Troubles. Yes: the play was truly the baptism.

The most obvious choice for the director would have been to set *Romeo and Juliet* in Northern Ireland, to have the lovers from across the religious divide—but he chose not to; it was much too obvious. He was God. We agreed with everything he thought.

Everything I am now is made from some dust of then.

I was taught the ephemeral nature of theatre. How no one performance is the same as the other. That each night, a world was brought to life, and the people in it, a story was played out and then it was all gone. I remember later, when I toured plays, that that sense was even clearer. On that long-ago run of *Romeo and Juliet*, we might exit the stage, the lights would go off, but the set remained—waiting for us to bring it to life again the next night. The set left there as a promise, a commitment to that world. Touring, the set was packed away every night, we left an empty stage for those that came behind, with new worlds, new people, new stories.

People Never Last
Susan McKay

'People are insubstantial,' murmured the doctor, as his bowler-hatted head drooped sleepily on to his chest. 'They never last. Of course, it makes no difference in the long run.'
—JG Farrell, *Troubles*

1.

I hear he's gone to some far country
And that he cares no more for me
—Jean Ritchie, 'My Dear Companion'

One night when I was driving through these mountains with my mother, we came around a twist in the road and saw in the middle of a boggy field a wooden rocking horse crazily spotlit by the silver blaze of a full moon. The place was called Scraghey, and it was a stretch of near-wilderness in County Tyrone, close to the border with County Donegal. There was a fast, tumbling river, a sign on the road indicating a path to a waterfall. I often thought of stopping, but never did, because the loneliness of the area had an uneasy edge.

I knew these roads. I passed through these places often on my route from Derry—where I am from and where my parents still lived then, in a house beside the River Faughan—to Fermanagh, to which I had recently moved. I knew that on the far side of this wilderness lay the town of Castlederg. But in my memory of those times, I leave that dark town unexplored to drive across an old stone bridge lit up by a Victorian street lantern and out on the road into County Fermanagh, where I lived alone in the gatelodge at Castle Coole, near Enniskillen.

My lovely house was surrounded by a park full of tall beech, chestnut and oak trees—and this was a charmed time in my life. I had escaped, or been banished from, a relationship with D, the writer with whom I had thought I would spend the rest of my days, though nothing in his history suggested that such permanence held any appeal for him. I had met him in Belfast in the early 1980s when I was working in the rape crisis centre, trying to help women recover from sexual violence that mostly included betrayal.

We had moved together south of the border, to the Glencar valley between Sligo and Leitrim, 'the waters and the wild' of Yeats's poem 'The Stolen Child'. A magical place: two waterfalls tumbled from mountain streams at the back of our house, wild birds sang, and the sun rose across the lake. But we had trailed our damage with us. He drank like a fish, said he wanted to break me. Our moments of sweetness became rarer and rarer. We ruined everything.

My mother did not hide her relief when this relationship finally ended and I moved back to the North and to Castle Coole in 1988. I got a job supporting community groups along the border. She loved to come and stay with me at the gatelodge, gathering sticks in the woods to light the fire, planting my garden. My mother's handbag contained a rarely used lipstick and a pair of secateurs. She knew the Latin names of every plant and flower, wild or cultivated. She said if she ever lost her memory these would be the last words to go.

It was 1988, less than a year after the IRA had bombed the Remembrance Day ceremony at Enniskillen, killing eleven people and injuring many others as they commemorated those from the area who had fought and died in two World Wars. I passed the bombsite on my way to work. In my personal state of euphoria, I did not fully grasp at first that the town was still in shock. I did not know that the woman who ran the shop where I bought flamboyant summer dresses had lost both her parents in the bomb.

I learned at this time that each small border village was actually two, each shadowing the other, vigilant, fearful. There were army checkpoints on all the roads. A major from the Ulster Defence Regiment stood at my hedge as I deadheaded my geraniums and told me that if the police had shot the rioters back in 1969 it would have never got this bad. I gathered honeysuckle, padlocked the gate of the estate at night and sat on my sandstone steps listening to *La Traviata*.

A poet I had known from the life before called one day with a folded page from my former lover. It was photocopied from a book of poems by Brodsky, who had written a dedication on it to the two of us. We had met him when he read in Belfast. I had attempted awkwardly through the fog of my cigarette smoke to tell him how terrifying the city was for the people in the harshest and most violent districts.

> She folds her memories like a parachute....
> I dream of her either loved or killed
> Because the town's too small.

There was no other message from D and I sent none back. He was already living with someone else by then, while writing a novel in which a woman like a punished ghost of me is loved and lost by a man like a tormented ghost of him. A gentle and understanding woman waits in the shadows to rescue him. It was a pattern I should have recognised from the novel he was writing when I met him. After I left, or he left—I really don't know which—I saw him rarely; though our eyes met, we never spoke. The last time was at a funeral. I arrived late and had driven so fast I almost crashed. He was intoning, '... and death shall have no dominion.'

2.

Come away, O human child! To the waters and the wild…
—WB Yeats, 'The Stolen Child'

I lived for a healing year at Castle Coole, and then I moved to Dublin and began to work as a journalist. I met and fell in love with a man who loved me back. Our daughters were born. Life steadied and was exciting.

In 1994, a tragic story brought me back to Castlederg, and to that lonesome wilderness to its west. Arlene Arkinson was missing. Family photos were published showing a smiling girl with sparkling eyes. The fifteen-year-old had last been seen alone in a car with Robert Howard, aged 55 and with a string of rape convictions behind him. In 1993, a friend of Arlene had escaped Howard by jumping from the upstairs window of a sordid house in which he kept caged birds. Half dressed, bruised and terrified, Priscilla ran through the town to the heavily fortified compound which houses the police station.

Castlederg was a town still at war, though elsewhere peace talks were inching towards ceasefires. Partition in 1921 had made it inevitable that the border region was going to fail to thrive. Castlederg, like other towns in Tyrone, Fermanagh and Donegal, had ended up on the frayed edges of the new states, the new border zigzagging along streams, through bogs, over mountains. These towns, remote from both Belfast and Dublin, were now cut off from their economic hinterlands. The railways that used to connect them were allowed to decline and by the middle of the 1960s had all been abandoned.

Then, in 1969, the Troubles began. The roads into Castlederg were for a time sealed off, and there were regular pitched battles between factions from either end of the town. The IRA bombed the town and killed local Protestants, some of them members of the security forces. A Protestant minister said to me once of two IRA men killed there by the British Army: 'I wouldn't drop a lot of tears for them.'

Priscilla felt she was not taken seriously by the police. She felt unbelieved. When her case came to court, Howard was given bail: a wolf in wolf's clothing, he was allowed to roam. His target was girls and young women who appeared lost, unprotected, already violated. He sought out poor, neglected areas, and people who were marginalised within them; and he fetched up in Castlederg.

Her mother's death when Arlene Arkinson was eleven, left her lonely and adrift. She lived between the homes of her siblings, fighting them as they tried to impose boundaries and keep her safe. A man sexually abused her. She drank in Castlederg's bars. She was afraid of the dark. Her teachers said she had promise but was too often absent. She and her friends who were out on the edge— and Howard had his eye on them.

One night in the summer of 1994, he drove Arlene,

another girl and her older boyfriend across the border that runs along the river Derg at Pettigo. There's a statue in the town commemorating IRA men killed fighting British forces in 1922: the 'Quiet Man', as he is known, points his rifle across the river into the North. The road passes through darkly regimented state forestry, beyond which lies Lough Derg, the site of an island to which Catholic pilgrims go to do penance for their sins. A cave on the island is believed to be the entrance to purgatory: this is the border between life and life everlasting; or life, death and damnation.

Howard drove on through Donegal to the Atlantic resort of Bundoran. They drank in the Palace Hotel: then, in the early hours, Howard dropped the others off at a house in Scraghy and drove off with Arlene. A coroner's report in 2021 found that he had in all likelihood murdered her and disposed of her body within hours, probably on the Northern Ireland side of the border. The police did not move to intercept Howard, and soon afterwards, he was driven out of Castlederg by the IRA to a van across the border. He went to Scotland, then England, where in 2002 he murdered fourteen-year-old Hannah Williams. This time Howard was caught and convicted—but a subsequent attempt to prosecute him for Arlene's murder failed.

The Arkinson family was desperate to lay Arlene to rest in a grave, and local people, police and experts searched acres of lakes, rivers, forests and bogs for her remains. Howard refused to help—but in any case, it is difficult to find a body in a wilderness. Further along the Tyrone border, Columba McVeigh, one of those the IRA 'disappeared', is also missing, even though detailed information was provided to the commission tasked with finding him.

Because this is a landscape that changes. Most plants are scoured away by wind and rain—those that survive are tough. Near one such burial place, a tree has all but devoured a string of rosary beads left by a searching family.

3.

The bogholes might be Atlantic seepage,
The wet centre is bottomless.
—Seamus Heaney, 'Bogland'

The writer Garrett Carr walked through these borderlands when researching his book *The Rule of the Land*, and described the extreme desolation both of the place and of the state of mind it induced in him. 'I might,' he writes, 'be the only person to walk this way in weeks but this does not make it an adventure, I just feel I'm making a mistake. I don't mean I've misread the map, it takes a deeper kind of failure to end up on this barren bog, cold, unsure and far from society.' Yet this land can also be loved fiercely—in her novel *Big Girl, Small*

Town, Michelle Gallen describes a landscape her heroine's troubled family have 'clung to for generations'.

In November 2020 this border landscape moved. Thousands of tons of viscous black bogland slid: a mass of watery land surging devastatingly from west to east, from Donegal into Tyrone. I arranged to meet a couple of local environmentalists at one of the border bridges: they described seeing a long black peaty veil spreading itself across a swathe of land between forests. I could see uprooted trees ditched like so many broken umbrellas. Thick black acidic water coursed into the rivers Mourne and Derg—salmon rivers, now fouled—and the dark and intense smell of the disturbed earth lingering in the air. Vast amounts of sequestered carbon had now been released into the atmosphere.

Of course, the signs had been there to see. A few years back, a section of new forestry road had sunk into the swamp. 'The earth up there is just sitting on water,' one of the group said. 'It's all wee lakes that have just been grown over.' Everyone knew the land was unstable, another said. 'There is an ancient lake up there under the bog and if you touch it the bog begins to move.' A developer was building a windfarm in the bog, which had already suffered from intense spruce forestry and road construction. And now, 'The wind turbines are mounted on blocks of wire and concrete,' said one of the activists. 'There was digging and blasting going on for months. The bog has to go somewhere.'

Some local people had protested at what they saw as the reckless exploitation of this fragile environment; others sold land to the forestry bodies and to the wind-farm developers. 'You have no idea what this does to a community,' one of the activists said. They asked not to be named. 'You'd just be afraid nearly to say anything.' I spoke with an environmentalist named Catherine. 'It seems like there is an assumption that this is just a useless old bog and you can do what you want with it,' she said. 'Throw your old sofa into it. Stick a windfarm on it, plant a forest. The landscape has no voice. It is like women in abusive relationships. Nature has no voice. And the people who know the land are not listened to and they get disheartened.'

While I was in the area I met a woman who was walking along the road. Sarah loves this place. The bog slippage had covered what used to be her father's sheep grazing land. She remembered when there were hen harriers in the skies. 'Massive big beautiful birds,' she said. 'And they had a beautiful cry too.' She pointed out the house of her grandmother Cecily Meehan, whose mixed Protestant and Catholic name captures the nature of this community before the partition of Ireland. 'She had a border shop,' Sarah said, 'and there was great craic at it selling flour and lemonade and raisins and coffee and tea, all the stuff that was cheaper in the North. Then the Troubles came. British soldiers put steel spikes across the road, and when locals dug them out, the army blew up the road and left deep craters that soon filled up with water. The formerly mixed community was divided: Sarah pointed out the ruins of houses that were abandoned.

Sarah remembers Robert Howard hiding out in this border area after he killed Arlene. One day a friend called her and said she'd seen him at a local takeaway. 'I was on my own in the house and I walked into my daughter's bedroom—there was a toy dinosaur in there that opened its mouth and roared when you came close to it. I ran out of the house terrified and jumped in the car and just drove,' she said.

She introduced me to John, another local, and I visited him during a spate of wild, deluging rain. The rivers were in flood and driving the twisty back roads sent waves of spray into the hedges. Conflict had never been far away in the border region: John recalled his father talking about British soldiers from the feared Black and Tans militia at the time of partition. 'They'd have disturbed the thatch looking for guns. My father kept his shotgun buried in a foalskin.' He said as a boy he and his friends used to find rusted rifles hidden in ditches by old IRA men. There were wallsteads near his house of an old prison run by the IRA. 'At one stage,' he says, 'we were taking up spuds and I found a sword.'

His wife Marian, spoke of more recent times. 'My father had a wetland area called the meadows,' she says, 'and we found rifles hidden in the rush bushes and one time there was a lorry bomb primed at the back of the house.' The couple recalled IRA volunteers on the roads, British soldiers in the ditches. When the helicopter flew along the border, 'You could have picked needles off the street in the spotlights,' John said. 'There was always a fear on you,' Marian added.

When I left their house it was still pouring and darkness had fallen, and within minutes I was lost. With no phone signal, I had no choice but just to drive on until I reached a signpost. It directed me to Castlederg. It was not where I wanted to go, but I was glad when I reached its lights.

4.

Death's is a private country, / like love's.
—Moya Cannon, 'Death'

The house in which I grew up was just a few fields away from the River Faughan. When my father was dying, over a decade ago now, neighbours brought my mother a wild salmon caught from the river. Its skin was bright shining silver. The Faughan flows into the Foyle outside Derry, joining the north-flowing waters of the other rivers. The Strule becomes the Mourne, and the Derg flows into it, and the Mourne joins the Finn and becomes the Foyle, and that great river widens as it curves and passes under the bridges at Derry, which has its own border griefs. Derry's river and bridges are patrolled by the kind souls of the search and rescue team, who try to rescue people who come to the river with suicide in mind. 'I'm away to the river,' people say: and the phrase has a desperate meaning in this place.

The river at last spreads itself dazzlingly out under vast north-westerly skies into Lough Foyle, with Donegal on the west side, Derry on the east. The border disappears here: ownership of the lough has been disputed in various court cases involving the British and Irish governments; today, the matter has been left in limbo. But Lough Foyle is in no jurisdiction. It is as free as the swans and geese that gather in winter on the broad fields it floods. Its wide mouth opens and pours its waters into the Atlantic.

In his book *Room for the River*, Liam Campbell writes that Lough Foyle is the legendary burial place of Manannán Mac Lír, Celtic sea god and god of the underworld. He discusses the dispute over the ownership of a hoard of gold from 100 BC discovered in 1903 by a farmer at Broighter on the lough shore. Ownership of the gold depended on whether the hoard was deposited in the lough as a ritual offering to Manannán, or buried on land: but there is no certainty as to whether the area was above or below the lough—for this is a liminal place, what Campbell calls a 'thin place' where there is 'less of a barrier between heaven and earth.' The Broighter gold is now in the National Museum in Dublin. Its most exquisite item is a tiny gold boat with a mast, oars and benches.

My mother has dementia now and is drifting between life and oblivion. She is in a care home there at Broighter. There are no Latin flower names now. One day she seemed perplexed by something she did not understand outside the window of her room. She waved her hands to show me, and I saw the wind tossing the leaves of the trees in the grounds. 'Trees,' I said. 'Those are trees.' But her fragmented thoughts had unmoored from the trees by then. Sometimes I list the names of the dogs she owned over many years and she seems pleased to hear of them. I hope she does not remember the Troubles, or the loss of the husband she loved for half a century, or the times her daughters drove her to shout and weep. I would like her to remember the moonlight on the rocking horse.

In John Montague's long meditative poem 'Border Sick Call', he accompanies his brother, a doctor, on a series of visits to elderly patients living in the remote 'lost lands', the mountainy boglands of Tyrone. There is chat about the border and smuggling and guns. 'Hereabouts, signs are obliterated,' the poem begins. The poet's brother informs him that 'the real border is not between / countries, but between life and death...'—but the poet is not convinced.

My mother is neither living nor dead. She believed in neither heaven nor hell and although her present condition seems to me like purgatory, I am not sure she had ever heard of it. I wish the golden Broighter boat could bear her gently away out into the ocean and let her go.

I know I'm not normal but I'm trying to change
Susannah Dickey

The first moment of quasi-sexual intimacy in *Muriel's Wedding* (1994) sees Muriel writhing on a bean bag with Brice Nobes, a parking inspector ('I have to tell you something,' he says, 'I'm a parking inspector'). The relatable clumsiness of the moment mutates into something maniacal as Brice lowers himself to a crouch and motorboats Muriel, while she, unaccustomed to such passion, cackles. He accidentally unzips the beanbag, rather than her trousers, then tries to unclothe her. He falls back, knocking a birdcage through a window. The newly permitted breeze flurries the white beans from the beanbag, and two other men appear in the doorway, both naked. They've heard Muriel's squealing and have rushed to her aid. One of the men apprehends Brice while the other attends to Muriel, who is still laughing. Rhonda, her best friend, appears in the doorway. She falls to the floor. 'Mariel (sp),' she says quietly, 'I can't move my legs.' Cut to: ambulance.

The first time I saw the film adaptation of *Mamma Mia* (2008) was in the cinema on the Strand Road, Derry.

The second time I saw it was the day I was head-butted in the face. Cut to: police station.

★

Every year on a late September Thursday, my school had a prize night. My former school is the one (ostensibly) mixed-denomination grammar school in Derry, although it veered majority Protestant, and the school's practices in many regards were incontrovertibly Protestant, or unionist—we said the Protestant version of the Lord's Prayer; we sang the British national anthem at school events (the aforementioned prize night was one such event, if I remember correctly). Anyway, after the prize night, it was customary to go to Earth, which at the time was the less salubrious of Derry's two fairly insalubrious night clubs. The following school day was always abbreviated, probably to let the sixth-form students, as well as the teachers, recover from their hangovers. Half days at school always felt unduly prodigious: we got to wear something other than our misshapen uniforms; we were dispatched from the grounds at lunchtime.

I was sixteen years old, three weeks shy of seventeen. That Friday I walked into town with my friends, intent on buying a dress that might consolidate my more indecorous fantasies. My school was, at the time, on what we call the city side or west side of the River Foyle (it has since moved across to the east side of the city) and that afternoon we followed the Northland Road, swung a left onto Rock Road, then a right onto the Strand Road. We walked past Earth, Domino's, Houston Shoes, Suede hair salon. It was a nice day, relative to Derry— not cold. We were ebullient, dressed in our best outfits. It was somewhere between the Magee campus of Ulster University and the Queen's Quay roundabout that I heard someone say, 'Are you laughing at me?'

Lacking spatial awareness, or much sense of self-preservation, I had failed to notice the man walking towards us. Now, he was close, and he was addressing me. 'Are you laughing at me?' I looked at him. I think I said, 'What?' and he said, again, 'Are you fucking laughing at me?' He was very close now. I think I said, 'No,' and he said 'You were fucking laughing at me.' He took a step closer, I a step back. He steered me like a sheepdog, not making contact, all the while saying, 'You were laughing at me, you were laughing at me.' He cordoned me from the rest of the group, waltzed me. His head remained a few centimetres from my own—a proximity and an intimacy that would have been a bit much even without the mounting threat. Soon, my back was against the wall that runs alongside the pavement, and then—in my memory it's sort of a low-pitched, echo-y badum—his forehead collided with the bridge of my nose and my head reverberated off the wall. The immediate aftermath was sort of placid: I stood there, blinking. My friends stood there, blinking. He exited.

A car, going past at that moment, pulled up. An indeterminate number of young men got out and gave chase. They caught up with the man fairly quickly, and then they had him on the ground. A few of my bolder friends tentatively approached the throng: I remember hearing one of them yell 'Bastard!' at the short, bald man in the grey hoodie, now a bit bloodied. I still hadn't moved, wasn't done blinking. Another friend phoned the police and then they were there, too. The man was chaperoned away, the young men were—I don't know, but I think they required urgent hospital treatment, for reasons I learned about later. I was delivered to the police station. I was told afterwards that, while he was on the ground, my assailant repeated the word 'Fenians'. (Of those of us who were there, I think one was Catholic. This compares with another afternoon, about a year before, when a man muttered 'Fucking huns' at three of us, as we walked up Waterloo Street in our uniforms. On that occasion, two out of three of us were Catholic.)

That evening, another friend, Laura, who hadn't been there to bear witness, was hosting a screening of *Mamma Mia* at her house. I have no explanation for why this was happening other than the fact that we were all really into *Mamma Mia*. The afternoon had been a bit frenetic—I gave a statement at the police station; my mother came, fraught but measured; my father took me to see a doctor, who kneaded my nose between his hands and told me there was some risk of a hairline fracture and

I should avoid sneezing (I may be misremembering that interaction). My mother suggested I might not want to go to the *Mamma Mia* party, but I never entertained not going. I put on some fresh leggings and a fresh cardigan and I went. I spent the night at my friend's house and the next day I returned home, puffy-faced and slightly black-eyed, to a gift from a friend who lived two streets away, but who had heard a gently, but tellingly, distorted version of what had happened: that I had been the victim of a sectarian attack. The gift was two teddy bears of different colours, their arms and paws sewn together in a forever hug.

★

In September 2019 I watched *Muriel's Wedding* for the first time and I realised that a decade had passed since I'd last seen *Mamma Mia*, and since being head-butted. *Muriel's Wedding*, similarly to *Mamma Mia*, is a film built around the music of ABBA. However, their cohabitation of this niche is an uneasy one.

Muriel's Wedding is a film a little about friendship, a lot about cathexis, and a lot about having to come to terms with the more unsavoury elements of your own character, and your environment. Muriel, an Australian teenager, is obsessed with marriage: desperate for it, hungry for it. However, her looks, her socioeconomic status, and her off-putting mannerisms, make this seem an unobtainable dream. The music of ABBA offers her respite from her unhappy circumstances. While Donna Sheridan, Tanya Chesham-Leigh and Rosie Mulligan (three of the protagonists of *Mamma Mia*) lead an eclectic crew of island locals and hotel staff onto a pier while singing 'Dancing Queen', Muriel, of *Muriel's Wedding*, murmurs along to her ABBA tape, having been escorted home from the wedding of Tania—another Tania, the film's principal antagonist—under suspicion of shoplifting. While Sophie Sheridan's wedding becomes filibustered by her paternal curiosities, Muriel stands dolefully at the window with a stolen wedding bouquet, watching her ethically questionable father wave to the departing police. ABBA, so intrinsic to the wide-eyed optimism of *Mamma Mia*, serves to reinforce Muriel's own unhappy circumstances.

Superficially, Muriel might not seem so dichotomous from the chipper buoyancy of the *Mamma Mia* lifestyle. Muriel wants friendship, laughter, a sexy soon-to-be-husband, and choreography. That said, her moral ambivalence and mercenary pursuits of her dream have no place in the ABBA dreamscape: she steals from her parents, lies relentlessly, reneges on promises, and, following Rhonda's diagnosis with a spinal-cord tumour, decamps to a bridal shop. Rhonda seemingly now absent from her thoughts, she stares at a mannequin, its arm up in a gesture of hieratic blessing. A choral rendition of 'Dancing Queen' plays.

Muriel's Wedding is a film that is never not mocking its characters. In a deserted Emergency Room a sign reads: 'Waiting time for non-urgent patients is now: 2 hours'. Tania, knowing that Chook, her husband, has been receiving fellatio from someone else, maintains: 'Marrying him was the happiest day of my life'. Betty Heslop, Muriel's long-suffering mother, cuts a phone call short with, 'I have to go—we're being raided again.'

It is a film with a relentlessly nihilistic worldview, the ABBA catalogue an aegis held up by the bloodthirsty Muriel, forever trying to keep at bay the reality of herself: 'I won't go back to being her!' While *Mamma Mia*'s Sophie Sheridan is crawling languorously across the sand, salted and sexy, singing 'Lay all your love on me', Muriel is saying to Rhonda, following Rhonda's futile attempts at rehabilitative physiotherapy: 'When I lived in Porpoise Spit I'd just stay in my room for hours and listen to ABBA songs. Sometimes I'd stay in there all day. Since I met you and moved to Sydney I haven't listened to one ABBA song. It's because now my life's as good as an ABBA song. It's as good as Dancing Queen.' Donna Sheridan, the all-singing, all-powerful matriarch of *Mamma Mia*, makes for an unkind contrast to the Betty of *Muriel's Wedding*, who endures belittlement, rejection, and eventually, death. It is a film that has little by way of didacticism: there is a quasi-happy ending, but it comes after Muriel has made countless, countless errors. Ultimately, the film suggests, little means anything, but everything might turn out sort of fine.

Mamma Mia is a film of incorrigible positivity, a-capitalist euphoria and self-acceptance (upon seeing several of her quite good pencil sketches, prospective father Sam Carmichael tells Sophie, 'You should pursue this', as if art is a career option for anyone with a dream). It is also a film with a simple, formulaic approach to narrative: here is the plot's one source of tension and conflict, here's how it is easily resolved (through love, acceptance, understanding). *Muriel's Wedding*, on the other hand, happens in a pecuniary-obsessed metropolis, with racism and classism going untampered. It just about manages some final act of redemption, but after considerable expense to both Muriel and Rhonda. It berates its more likable characters' idealism and punishes them for wanting.

Perhaps, most importantly, it is also a film that makes much of heads. So much of the camera work prioritises heads: we chase after Muriel's crown as she strides into Breakers bar; we are seated somewhere in the crowd while she and Rhonda dance to 'Waterloo'. The camera pans slowly leftwards, and our view gets interrupted by out-of-focus shoulders and permed hair. Many of the conversations occur at eye level, or just below eye-level and we, the viewer, are rarely taller than the tallest person in the shot. In fact, we are often held at an ignoble crotch height.

During Muriel and Rhonda's dance to 'Waterloo' on Hibiscus Island we experience a discomfiting propinquity;

their perpendicular choreography oscillates between their side-profiles, and straight-to-camera unabashed staring. Compare this to the 'Waterloo' post-credits scene of *Mamma Mia*: the characters have gained access to some sort of boundless amphitheatre, unencumbered by the tedium of architecture or atmosphere or narrative cogency. Where is this well-lit proscenium, with its sublime acoustics and pyrotechnics? Donna breaks the fourth wall to ask us, raspily, 'Do you want another one? Do you want another one?' As with 'Are you laughing at me? Are you fucking laughing at me?', it seems like there's no answer that might alter the outcome. Resignedly, we submit to another one.

In contrast, the cinematography in *Muriel's Wedding* is claustrophobic, and we are always made to feel either a little complicit, or a lot prey to the film's farce and futility. With its use of perspective it asks us to place ourselves in the shoes of its various characters, who remain messy and unknowable. Watching it again, recently, I was reminded of the man's head, too close to my own, of what he shouted afterward—who did he think he was hurting? Did he think he had successfully thwarted a cultural, ideological adversary? At the time I thought it was funny: what he said, how he'd got it so wrong, how I wasn't what he thought I was. Now, I think it's more discomfiting—these markers of identity have neither dissolved into arbitrary meaninglessness, nor are they indicators of a straightforward binary. Instead, they are entrenched within a wider, more important context of class that I think is failing to be addressed, as fruitless discussions of the 'binary' continue to dominate certain conversations. The social mobility that was on offer to my parents' generation, and from which my father and aunt benefited (that my uncle was able to benefit only to an extent, was an indicator of how throwing money at a problem is not necessarily a panacea to all social and cultural traps) has not solved anything.

As the man on the pavement stared at me, our closeness was such I was conscious of being able to look in only one of his eyes at a time; an enforced impotence that *Muriel's Wedding*'s camera work achieves also. I know so little about him, about what led him to be so desperate to return to Magilligan prison (where he had just come from) that he assaulted a teenage girl. In what way did the narrative fail him? *Muriel's Wedding* is a film that focuses on the individual, on the challenges of personal circumstance. It is also a film that addresses the unknowability of the other, the small contained-ness of individual experience. Contrast this with the establishing shots and glorious panoramas of the Sheridans' multi-sensory extravaganza, where we are often sky-bound, disembodied, insignificant but also omnipresent, subject to some wider, apotheosis of pathos.

When I was sixteen, I wanted all the things that (presumably) lots of sixteen-year-olds want: to be well-dressed, to be thought beautiful. On that September day in Derry, in a way that I hadn't been made explicitly aware of before, I was also subject to my surroundings, in a way that sat somewhat incompatibly with my aspirations. I had the fervent lascivious yearnings of Muriel Heslop, and also her bathos of circumstance. What I wanted, that day, was winsome merriment (and a dress that might finally make someone want to shag me). What I got, instead, was a faceful of man's forehead. A man who, it transpired, had assaulted another woman immediately prior to our encounter, and who was also HIV positive. Had 'Gimme Gimme Gimme' been layered over the events, the whole thing could have been a *Muriel's Wedding* outtake: a chaotic afternoon, a paean to caprice and meaninglessness.

★

I was asked, not long ago, if I could be tempted to contribute to a piece that hoped to examine why writers from Derry leave Derry at the first opportunity. Ultimately, I felt unable to participate, for the same reason I bristle a little when writers from other parts of the UK attempt to précis the situation in Northern Ireland: because I think by either mythologising a place erroneously, or by simplifying its circumstances, by casting it as either some inverted Tír na nÓg, or as some turbulent place of ideological conflict, we infantilise it, we fail to hold it to the same standards as we do elsewhere. You might leave Derry for the same reasons you might leave anywhere—to extricate yourself from parental influence, to explore your gender or sexuality, to seek greater opportunities of work and culture. You also might leave Derry for the same reasons you might specifically leave the north of Ireland—not because of the Troubles, but because of its racism, its transphobia, its appalling dearth of reproductive rights.

At the time, getting head-butted was the most interesting thing that had ever happened to me. It was also, with hindsight, the worst thing, but it had little, I believe, to do with my perceived belonging to one denomination, regardless of what the man on the ground was shouting. It is for this reason that I have decided to spend so much of this essay talking about *Muriel's Wedding*: because I believe there is no easily resected topic of 'Northern Ireland', and if there is, it's not one I feel equipped to tackle. It is a place that suffers from a combination of misunderstandings, and logocentric mythologising. I am wary of attempting to describe what it is like, because to do so perpetuates some idea that there is any homogeneity of experience. As part of the so-named 'post-conflict generation', I can only speak to how it was for me. I can't even have a go at attempting to speak for those I was close to, because, by virtue of Northern Ireland not having a dominant private-school infrastructure, my friends were from widely varying socio-economic backgrounds, and it is that, more than anything, that will reflect experience. I will say that it was deeply symptomatic of my adolescence to be largely ignorant of the wider political environment in which I found myself. I'm sure this is true of others, growing up middle class. I'm not sure if my ignorance was a by-product of my parents enabling it (I'm sure it was true that many families sought to shield their children from certain contexts) or whether it was a wilful, petulant rejection of their attempts to educate me (knowing myself, it was more likely the latter). Regardless, I grew up with the basest grasp of how things were, of how things had been. Mine was not a childhood / adolescence pocked by the residue of the conflict, and this was a privilege I'm sure many of my generation will be familiar with. (What is strange, however, is that my familial history is not void of direct exposure and involvement, but I was unaware of this until only very, very recently).

What happened to me that day was less, whatever the story that was circulated afterwards, a sectarian-based violence than it was a gendered one. Northern Ireland, I think, increasingly, risks being subsumed by its own narrative, by the idea that its problems continue to be those of fifty years ago. The more we perpetuate these ideas the more reductive any discussions of Northern Ireland will be. The instances of violence we are seeing now are the fault of systemic class inequality. Northern Ireland's biggest problems are the same problems of everywhere else: poverty, racism, misogyny, homophobia, transphobia, the climate crisis. It also has specific, localised problems that are not served by the idea that its animosities are neatly contained within its borders: for example, the continued no-holding-to-account of British soldiers. While the Six Counties continue to have inflicted upon them the straw man of 'The Troubles' or of Brexit, these problems go ignored, unchallenged, unaddressed—we continue to be a misunderstood afterthought, neglected from wider conversations.

Events of our lives become tethered to arbitrary things, through accidents of shared temporality. I was watching Tim Burton's *Corpse Bride*, one Saturday morning in 2006, the day I found out my uncle was dead, the reasons for which are myriad but also, I believe, tethered to his history, his immediate location and his class status. I watched *Mamma Mia* on the day I got walloped, an act fuelled by infrastructural problems of poverty. A decade later, I watched *Muriel's Wedding*, and there is little to tether it to, except all of what I am, which is a messy product of a place which remains irreducible to one idea.

Contributors

BRIAN MCGILLOWAY is a writer from Derry. He is the author of twelve crime novels including the Ben Devlin mysteries; and the Lucy Black series. His writing has been shortlisted for a CWA Dagger and the Theakston's Old Peculier Crime Novel of the Year; and he has won the BBC Tony Doyle Award for his screenplay, *Little Emperors*. His novel, *The Last Crossing*, won Highly Commended in Theakston's Old Peculier Crime Novel of the Year 2021. Brian currently works as an English teacher in Strabane. His most recent novel is *The Empty Room*.

CARLO GÉBLER is a writer born in Dublin and now living in County Fermanagh. His most recent publications (all from New Island) include *The Innocent of Falkland Road*, a novel set in London in the 1960s, *Aesop's Fables, the Cruelty of the Gods* (a collaboration with the artist Gavin Weston), *Tales We Tell Ourselves,* a selection of stories from *Boccaccio's Decameron*, and *I, Antigone*, which purports to be Antigone's biography of her father, Oedipus. He teaches at the Oscar Wilde Centre for Irish Writing at Trinity College Dublin, and HMP Maghaberry. He is a member of Aosdana.

GAIL MCCONNELL is a poet and critic from Belfast, interested in violence, creatureliness, queerness and the possibilities and politics of language and form. She is the author of *The Sun is Open* (Penned in the Margins, 2021), *Fothermather* (Ink Sweat & Tears, 2019), *Fourteen* (Green Bottle Press, 2018) and *Northern Irish Poetry and Theology* (Palgrave, 2014). *The Sun is Open* won the John Pollard Foundation International Poetry Prize 2022 and is shortlisted for the Christopher Ewart-Biggs Memorial Prize.

HENRIETTA MCKERVEY was born in Belfast and now lives in Dublin. She is the author of four novels: *A Talented Man* (2020); *Violet Hill* (2018); *The Heart of Everything* (2016); and *What Becomes Of Us* (2015). She holds a Hennessy First Fiction Award and was the winner of the inaugural UCD Maeve Binchy Travel Award. In 2021 she and artist Stephanie Sloan created *Daybreak in the Land of Statues*, a specially commissioned artwork for the National Library of Ireland. She is a regular contributor to the *Irish Independent* and RTÉ radio.

JAN CARSON is a writer and community arts facilitator based in Belfast. She specialises in engagement with older people. She has published three novels, two micro-fiction collections, and two short story collections. Her novel *The Fire Starters* won the EU Prize for Literature for Ireland 2019. Jan also won the Harper's Bazaar Short Story Competition (2016) and was shortlisted for the BBC National Short Story Award (2020) and An Post

Irish Short Story of the Year (2021). Her work has been translated into multiple languages. Jan's latest novel, *The Raptures* was published by Doubleday in early 2022.

KERRI NÍ DOCHARTAIGH was born and raised in Derry. She is the author of *Thin Places* (Canongate, 2020) which was highly commended by the Wainwright Prize for Nature Writing 2021. She has written for the Guardian, the Irish Times, the BBC, Winter Papers, and others. Her second book, *Cacophony of Bone*, is forthcoming in April 2023.

Poet and creative producer MARIA MCMANUS was born in Enniskillen and now lives in Belfast. She founded the not-for-profit company 'Quotidian—Word on the Street', which creates innovative ways to animate civic space with literature. Quotidian's inaugural project was to create Ireland's first Poetry JukeBox, located at The Crescent Arts Centre in Belfast. Maria's books include *Available Light* (Arlen House 2018), *We are Bone* (Lagan Press 2013), *The Cello Suites* (Lagan Press, 2009) and *Reading the Dog* (Lagan Press 2006).

NANDI JOLA is a South African-born poet, writer and playwright. She is the 2022 Smock Alley Theatre Rachel Baptiste Award recipient; her one-woman play *The Journey* opened the International Literature Festival Dublin in 2021; and she represented the Arts Council of Northern Ireland at the Transpoesie Poetry Festival in

Brussels. Nandi was a Mentor on the 21 Artists for the 21st Century Centenary programme by NIO; and is currently a Mentor for Doire Press Mentorship programme. Her new book is entitled *Home is Neither Here Nor There*. She lives in Belfast.

NEIL HEGARTY is a writer from Derry. His novels include *The Jewel*, published in 2019 and *Inch Levels*, which was shortlisted for the Kerry Group Novel of the Year award in 2017. Other titles include *Frost: That Was the Life That Was,* a biography of David Frost; and *The Story of Ireland*, which accompanies a BBC-RTE television history of Ireland. His essays and short fiction have appeared in the *Dublin Review, Stinging Fly, Tangerine* and elsewhere and he is a regular literary reviewer for the *Irish Times* and *Dublin Review of Books.*

PAUL MCVEIGH grew up in Belfast. His debut novel, *The Good Son*, won The Polari First Novel Prize and McCrea Literary Award, and was shortlisted for many others, including the Prix de roman Cezam. His short stories have appeared in numerous anthologies, journals and newspapers, and have been broadcast on BBC Radios 3, 4 and 5 Live, and Sky Arts. Paul is editor of the *Queer Love* anthology and *The 32: An Anthology of Irish Working Class Voices*; a co-founder of the London Short Story Festival; and an associate director of Word Factory.

SUSAN MCKAY is a writer and journalist from Derry. She has won many awards for her work, particularly on the legacy of political conflict. Her books include *Northern Protestants—On Shifting Ground* (Blackstaff 2021), *Bear in Mind These Dead* (Faber, 2008), *Northern Protestants—An Unsettled People* (Blackstaff, 2000) and *Sophia's Story* (Gill and MacMillan, 1998). Her journalism appears in *the New Yorker*, *the London Review of Books*, *the Guardian*, *the New York Times* and *the Irish Times*. She is currently writing a book about borders for which she received an Arts Council NI major individual award.

SUSANNAH DICKEY is a writer from Derry. Her second poetry pamphlet, *genuine human values* (The Lifeboat, 2018) won the Vincent Buckley Poetry Prize, and her third, *bloodthirsty for marriage* (Bad Betty Press, 2020), received an Eric Gregory Award from the Society of Authors. Her poetry and fiction have appeared in the *White Review*, *Dublin Review*, and elsewhere; and her story 'Stuffed Peppers' was longlisted for the 2021 *Sunday Times* Short Story Prize. Susannah is the author of two novels: *Tennis Lessons* (Doubleday UK, 2020) and *Common Decency* (Doubleday, 2022).

Acknowledgements

The Centre Culturel Irlandais acknowledges with gratitude the support of the Department of Foreign Affairs, Culture Ireland, the Arts Council of Northern Ireland, and the British Council Northern Ireland. Without the vital support of each of these organisations, this book could not have been published.

The editors would like to thank the writers who have contributed to this book, as well as David Torrans and the team at No Alibis Press in Belfast, and the team at Centre Culturel Irlandais in Paris. Thanks also to John Lovett, Catherine Toal and Helen Lanigan Wood.

'Lighthouse Keeping' by Kay Ryan (from *Odd Blocks*, 2011) is reproduced by kind permission of Carcanet Press, Manchester, UK.

This book is dedicated to the late Ted Hickey, former Keeper of Art in the Ulster Museum, a keen supporter of No Alibis and of Irish writers and an integral part of the Northern Irish arts scene during the height of the Troubles.

An Roinn Gnóthaí Eachtracha
Department of Foreign Affairs

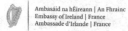
Ambasáid na hÉireann | An Fhrainc
Embassy of Ireland | France
Ambassade d'Irlande | France

Cultúr Éireann
Culture Ireland

BRITISH
COUNCIL

arts
council
of Northern Ireland